#MAKERS 4

ENGLISH ON THE MOVE

STUDENT'S BOOK

SERIES EDITOR:
IZAURA VALVERDE

Richmond

Richmond

Publishing Director: Sandra Possas

Editorial Manager: Izaura Valverde
Digital Content Manager: Adriana Pedro de Almeida

Design Coordinator: Raquel Buim

Senior Editors: Carina Guiname Shiroma, Giuliana Gramani
Editors: Lívia Mantovani, Márcia Nogueira, Sheila Saad, Veronica Teodorov Ferreira
Assistant Editor: Leila Scatena
Digital Content Editors: Ana Paula Campos, Cíntia Afarelli, Gabrielle Navarro, Priscila Oliveira Vieira, Thaís Tardivo
Contents: Camila Vilar, Daniele Crema, Gislaine Bonilha, Paulo Victor Dantas, Sandra Romani, Veronica Teodorov Ferreira, Vinicius Nobre
Copy Editors: Beatriz Simões, Flora Manzione, Helaine Albuquerque
Proofreaders: Carolina Waideman, Danielle Carvalho, Denise Cowle, Fernanda Bincoletto, Flora Manzione, Gabriele Martin Cândido, Katia Gouveia Vitale, Rafael Gustavo Spigel, Raura Monique Ikeda, Rich Rafterman, Vivian Cristina de Souza

Audio Production: Eastern Sky Media Services

Project Design: Amanda Miyuki, Rafael Gentile
Designers: Amanda Miyuki, Amanda Savoini, David Urbinatti (Teacher's Guide)
Digital Design Editors: Bruno Tersario, Daniel Favalli, Daniel Palmeira, Daniela Carrete, Eloah Cristina, Frodo Almeida, Mônica Oldrine, Roberto Ono
Digital Platform Development: Argeu Pereira da Ivenção (Technology Manager); Luiz Eduardo Mendes Duque (Technology Coordinator); Andrea Carina Pilipposian (Project Supervisor); Carolina Figueiredo (Project Analyst); Ana Paula Campos, Daniela Carrete, Eloah Cristina, Frodo Almeida (Concept Editors)
Educational Portal Content Editor: Sheila Rizzi
Layout: Casa de Ideias
Cover Design: Amanda Savoini
Cover Photos: Global_Pics/iStockphoto, walik/iStockphoto, Eshma/iStockphoto, dzubanovska/iStockphoto, kittiyaporn1027/iStockphoto
Artwork: Altair Sampaio, Amanda Miyuki, Amanda Savoini, Diego Lima, Karina de Sá, Manuel Miramontes, Priscila Wu, Rafael Gentile
Illustrations: Bruno Badain
Photo Researchers: Ellen Silvestre, Eveline Duarte, Mariana Zanato, Sara Alencar

Websites mentioned in this material were quoted for didactic purposes only. Richmond has no control over their content and urges care when using them.

Every effort has been made to trace the copyright holders, but if any omission can be rectified, the publishers will be pleased to make the necessary arrangements.

Impressão e acabamento: HRosa Gráfica e Editora
Lote: 287792

Dados Internacionais de Catalogação na Publicação (CIP)
(Câmara Brasileira do Livro, SP, Brasil)

#Makers : English on the move / editora responsável Izaura Valverde ; obra coletiva concebida, desenvolvida e produzida pela Editora Moderna. — 1. ed. — São Paulo : Moderna, 2018.

Obra em 4 v. para alunos do 6º ao 9º ano.

1. Inglês (Ensino fundamental) I. Valverde, Izaura.

18-16595 CDD-372.652

Índices para catálogo sistemático:
1. Inglês : Ensino fundamental 372.652
Iolanda Rodrigues Biode - Bibliotecária - CRB-8/10014

ISBN 978-85-16-11188-5 (LA)
ISBN 978-85-16-11189-2 (LP)

RICHMOND
EDITORA MODERNA LTDA.
Rua Padre Adelino, 758 — Belenzinho
São Paulo — SP — Brasil — CEP 03303-904
www.richmond.com.br
2020
Printed in Brazil

Photos: p. 8: metamorworks/iStockphoto, OKrasyuk/iStockphoto, PRImageFactory/iStockphoto, max-kegfire/iStockphoto; p. 9: Eloi_Omella/iStockphoto, KanKhem/iStockphoto, SolodkayaMari/iStockphoto; p. 10: bowie15/iStockphoto; p. 12: De Visu/Shutterstock; Geber86/iStockphoto; Igor Bulgarin/Shutterstock, 4 PM production/Shutterstock, Highwaystarz-Photography/iStockphoto, kostenkodesign/iStockphoto; p. 13: good_reason08/iStockphoto; p. 15: s_bukley/Shutterstock, Kathy Hutchins/Shutterstock, BBC; p. 19: mapasik/iStockphoto, gilaxia/iStockphoto, diane39/iStockphoto, bluebird13/iStockphoto; p. 20: Aleksei_Derin/iStockphoto; p. 21: oleg66/iStockphoto, Boykov/Shutterstock, kiruk/iStockphoto, Roberto Galan/iStockphoto; p. 22: benjaminec/Shutterstock; p. 24: nautiluz56/iStockphoto, Alina555/iStockphoto, LuminaStock/iStockphoto, rbv/iStockphoto, strickke/iStockphoto; p. 25: Suriyapong Thongsawang/iStockphoto, SerrNovik/iStockphoto, Juanmonino/iStockphoto; p. 28: brittak/iStockphoto, zmicier kavabata/Shutterstock, roccomontoya/iStockphoto, Deejpilot/iStockphoto; p. 29: southtownboy/iStockphoto, GOLFX/iStockphoto, dario hayashi/Shutterstock, jes2ufoto/iStockphoto; p. 30: justhavealook/iStockphoto, tzahiV/iStockphoto, AlbertPego/iStockphoto, majorosl/iStockphoto; p. 31: coldsnowstorm/iStockphoto, vector_s/iStockphoto; p. 34: Kozlik_Mozlik/iStockphoto, Son Hoang Tran/Shutterstock, ermess/iStockphoto, CREATISTA/iStockphoto; p. 35: VikiVector/iStockphoto, Hilch/Shutterstock; p. 36: wildpixel/iStockphoto; p. 38: HeForShe, MIGUEL ROJO/AFP, Rob Kim/Getty Images, HeForShe; p. 39: good_reason08/iStockphoto; p. 40: monkeybusinessimages/iStockphoto; p. 41: Kevin Mazur/Getty Images, Kathy Hutchins/Shutterstock, Science Source/Photoresearchers/Latinstock; p. 42: J Morc/Shutterstock; p. 44: praetorianphoto/iStockphoto, Steve Debenport/iStockphoto, slavemotion/iStockphoto, dimamorgan12/iStockphoto, g-stockstudio/iStockphoto, Geber86/iStockphoto; p. 48: francescoch/iStockphoto; p. 50: GlobalStock/iStockphoto, elenaleonova/iStockphoto, Neustockimages/iStockphoto, monkeybusinessimages/iStockphoto, damircudic/iStockphoto, amoklv/iStockphoto, zzorik/iStockphoto, Nottomanv1/iStockphoto, lutavia/iStockphoto; p. 51: Juanmonino/iStockphoto, OGphoto/iStockphoto, Svitlana Unuchko/iStockphoto, fstop123/iStockphoto; p. 52: VladimirFLoyd/iStockphoto, FatCamera/iStockphoto, SolisImages/iStockphoto, FatCamera/iStockphoto, stock-eye/iStockphoto, roshinio/iStockphoto; p. 54: Imgorthand/iStockphoto; p. 55: Wavebreakmedia/iStockphoto, nd3000/iStockphoto, kate_sept2004/iStockphoto, PhotoBylove/iStockphoto; p. 57: Steve Debenport/iStockphoto, taikrixel/iStockphoto; p. 59: bodnarchuk/iStockphoto; p. 60: fizkes/Shutterstock; p. 61: microgen/iStockphoto, Benevolente82/Shutterstock, torwai/iStockphoto, Bojan89/iStockphoto; p. 62: LoulouVonGlup/iStockphoto; p. 64: dimbar76/iStockphoto, CreativeFire/iStockphoto, marcoscisetti/iStockphoto, Wavebreakmedia/iStockphoto, molotovcoketail/iStockphoto; p. 65: Nikada/iStockphoto, Capuski/iStockphoto, kimrawicz/iStockphoto; p. 66: voyata/iStockphoto; p. 67: Betelgejze/iStockphoto, PieroAnnoni/iStockphoto, Tomas Abad/Alamy/Fotoarena, Everett - Art/Shutterstock, gremlin/iStockphoto, davidf/iStockphoto; p. 68: Nataniil/iStockphoto, Aleksei_Derin/iStockphoto, Cofeee/iStockphoto, a-wrangler/iStockphoto, valentinrussanov/iStockphoto, Yuri_Arcurs/iStockphoto; p. 69: humonia/iStockphoto; p. 70: AF-studio/iStockphoto, summerphotos/iStockphoto, JanakaMaharageDharmasena/iStockphoto, Drimafilm/iStockphoto; p. 71: Aleksei_Derin/iStockphoto, metamorworks/iStockphoto; p. 73: Niday Picture Library/Alamy/Fotoarena; p. 74: Anna Lshansky/Shutterstock; p. 76: AndreyPopov/iStockphoto; diego_cervo/iStockphoto, M_a_y_a/iStockphoto, martin-dm/iStockphoto, demaerre/iStockphoto, mikkelwilliam/iStockphoto; p. 78: courtneyk/iStockphoto, didecs/iStockphoto, Yurdakul/iStockphoto, gerenme/iStockphoto, simpson33/iStockphoto, stocknroll/iStockphoto, jmpaget/iStockphoto, JazzIRT/iStockphoto, Ivanko_Brnjakovic/iStockphoto, DmitriMaruta/iStockphoto, miriam-doerr/iStockphoto; p. 79: miriam-doerr/iStockphoto, image-stock.eu/Shutterstock, OstapandRoksolanaMykytiv/iStockphoto; p. 80: izusek/iStockphoto, coffeekai/iStockphoto, stevecoleimages/iStockphoto, image-stock.eu/Shutterstock, GaudiLab/iStockphoto, AndreyPopov/iStockphoto; p. 83: lolostock/iStockphoto, Morozov_photo/iStockphoto, stocknroll/iStockphoto, XiXinXing/iStockphoto, ljubaphoto/iStockphoto, AntonioGuillem/iStockphoto; p. 85: monkeybusinessimages/iStockphoto, andresr/iStockphoto, Halfpoint/iStockphoto, asiseeit/iStockphoto; p. 86: sabthai/Shutterstock, Byelikova_Oksana/iStockphoto, Pgiam/iStockphoto, burakkarademir/iStockphoto; p. 87: monkeybusinessimages/iStockphoto, bukharova/iStockphoto, onurdongel/iStockphoto; p. 88: Hayri Er/Getty Images; p. 90: andipantz/iStockphoto, martin-dm/iStockphoto; p. 91: mtreasure/iStockphoto, recep-bg/iStockphoto, CREATISTA/iStockphoto, SensorSpot/iStockphoto; p. 92: PanaceaArt/iStockphoto; p. 93: sbossert/iStockphoto, photographybyrobbie/iStockphoto, IDrazen_/iStockphoto; p. 94: Tyler Jump/IRC; p. 97: martin-dm/iStockphoto, Steve Debenport/iStockphoto, PeopleImages/iStockphoto; p. 99: heliopix/iStockphoto; p. 100: Dziggyfoto/iStockphoto; p. 102: AntonioGuillem/iStockphoto, TatyanaGl/iStockphoto, Tom Merton/iStockphoto, avdeev007/iStockphoto, Zephyr18/iStockphoto, Saro17/iStockphoto, seb_ra/iStockphoto; p. 103: pixelfit/iStockphoto, PeopleImages/iStockphoto, portishead1/iStockphoto, Ranta Images/iStockphoto; p. 104: sbeagle/iStockphoto, DGLimages/Shutterstock, Tyler Olson/Shutterstock, marcelmooij/iStockphoto, Ollyy/Shutterstock, Wavebreakmedia/iStockphoto, aiaimage/Paul Bradbury/Getty Images; p. 105: Syda Productions/Shutterstock, Alexander Supertramp/Shutterstock, metamorworks/iStockphoto, Vaclav Volrab/Shutterstock; p. 106: PR Image Factory/Shutterstock, manfredxy/iStockphoto, Metropolitan Museum of Art, New York, ablokhin/iStockphoto, antos777/iStockphoto, christopherhall/iStockphoto, Lorelyn Medina/Shutterstock; p. 107: Andyworks/iStockphoto, kopophoto/iStockphoto, sduben/iStockphoto, shanecotee/iStockphoto; p. 109: Krasula/Shutterstock, Eduardo_oliveros/iStockphoto, Choreograph/iStockphoto, Choreograph/iStockphoto, Geber86/iStockphoto, Mascha Tace/Shutterstock; p. 111: Evgenyi/Shutterstock, onurdongel/iStockphoto, Bridgeman/Fotoarena, Igor Bulgarin/Shutterstock; p. 112: hanohiki/iStockphoto, andresr/iStockphoto, Natnan Srisuwan/iStockphoto; p. 114: malerapaso/iStockphoto, Suradech14/iStockphoto, GrashAlex/iStockphoto, rasslava/iStockphoto, hocus-focus/iStockphoto; p. 115: DNKSTUDIO/iStockphoto, Floortje/iStockphoto; p. 116: Kaplanec/iStockphoto, Photosbyjam/iStockphoto, natrot/iStockphoto, Sezeryadigar/iStockphoto; p. 117: amnachphoto/iStockphoto, Kameleon007/iStockphoto, Korovin/iStockphoto, Serg_Velusceac/iStockphoto, empire331/iStockphoto, VvoeVale/iStockphoto, KariHoglund/iStockphoto, Coprid/iStockphoto, stanley45/iStockphoto; p. 120: piranka/iStockphoto, Berezko/iStockphoto, Gregory_DUBUS/iStockphoto, alexsokolov/iStockphoto; p. 126: martin-dm/iStockphoto, Pinkybird/iStockphoto, penguenstok/iStockphoto, dima_sidelnikov/iStockphoto; p. 128: SolStock/iStockphoto, omgimages/iStockphoto, marcoventuriniautieri/iStockphoto; p. 129: andresr/iStockphoto, cherry-hai/Shutterstock; p. 130: CagriOner/iStockphoto, Pom669/iStockphoto, liveslow/iStockphoto, Melnikof/iStockphoto; p. 131: tichr/iStockphoto, anouchka/iStockphoto, Bernard Barroso/Shutterstock, Supercel7/iStockphoto; p. 137: exdez/iStockphoto, Dan Gerber/Shutterstock; p. 138: lankogal/iStockphoto, Jose Gil/Shutterstock, FlairImages/iStockphoto, Kobby Dagan/Shutterstock, ermess/iStockphoto; p. 139: Paket/iStockphoto, Evgenii_Bobrov/iStockphoto; p. 141: Evan El-Amin/Shutterstock, rypson/iStockphoto, Studio-Pro/iStockphoto; p. 143: martin-dm/iStockphoto; p. 145: Christian Carollo/iStockphoto, invincible_bulldog/iStockphoto, rogkov/iStockphoto; p. 146: portishead1/iStockphoto, Hitdelight/Shutterstock; p. 147: RetroClipArt/Shutterstock, Ljupco/iStockphoto, evgenyatamanenko/iStockphoto, izusek/iStockphoto, GOLFX/iStockphoto, BrianAJackson/iStockphoto, SeanPavonePhoto/iStockphoto, everydayplus/iStockphoto; p. 148: XiXinXing/iStockphoto, kali9/iStockphoto, penguenstok/iStockphoto, ViDi Studio/iStockphoto, skhoward/iStockphoto, fstop123/iStockphoto, buzbuzzer/iStockphoto, taratata/iStockphoto; p. 149: VikiVector/iStockphoto, WorldWideImages/iStockphoto, HomoCosmicos/iStockphoto, 4kclips/Shutterstock, Sean Pavone/iStockphoto; p. 150: nialmi/iStockphoto; p. 151: littleny/iStockphoto, Marcelo-Kaneshira/iStockphoto, silverkblack/iStockphoto, kirza/iStockphoto, AntonioGuillem/iStockphoto; p. 152: KieselUndStein/iStockphoto, KevinHyde/iStockphoto, IakovKalinin/iStockphoto

Utilize este código QR para se cadastrar de forma mais rápida:

Ou, se preferir, entre em:

www.richmond.com.br/ac/livroportal

e siga as instruções para ter acesso aos conteúdos exclusivos do

Portal e Livro Digital

CÓDIGO DE ACESSO:

A 00131 MAKERS 4 13007

Faça apenas um cadastro. Ele será válido para:

MODERNA Richmond SANTILLANA ESPAÑOL

12111885 MAKERS 4 ON THE MOVE

From trees to books, sustainability all the way

Da semente ao livro, sustentabilidade por todo o caminho

Planting forests

The wood used as raw material for our paper comes from planted forests, that is, it is not the result of deforestation. This practice generates thousands of jobs for farmers and helps to recover environmentally degraded areas.

Plantar florestas

A madeira que serve de matéria-prima para nosso papel vem de plantio renovável, ou seja, não é fruto de desmatamento. Essa prática gera milhares de empregos para agricultores e ajuda a recuperar áreas ambientais degradadas.

Making paper and printing books

The entire paper production chain, from pulp production to book binding, is certified, complying with international standards for sustainable processing and environmental best practices.

Fabricar papel e imprimir livros

Toda a cadeia produtiva do papel, desde a produção de celulose até a encadernação do livro, é certificada, cumprindo padrões internacionais de processamento sustentável e boas práticas ambientais.

Creating content

Our educational solutions are developed with life-long goals guided by editorial values, diverse viewpoints and socio-environmental responsibility.

Criar conteúdos

Os profissionais envolvidos na elaboração de nossas soluções educacionais buscam uma educação para a vida pautada por curadoria editorial, diversidade de olhares e responsabilidade socioambiental.

Developing life projects

Richmond educational solutions are an act of commitment to the future of younger generations, enabling partnerships between schools and families in their mission to educate!

Construir projetos de vida

Oferecer uma solução educacional Richmond é um ato de comprometimento com o futuro das novas gerações, possibilitando uma relação de parceria entre escolas e famílias na missão de educar!

Richmond

Apoio: TWO SIDES www.twosides.org.br

Scan the QR code to learn more.
Access *richmond.com.br/quem-somos/praticas-sustentaveis/*

Fotografe o código QR e conheça melhor esse caminho.
Saiba mais em *richmond.com.br/quem-somos/praticas-sustentaveis/*

CONTENTS

SCOPE AND SEQUENCE

Unit	Topic	Vocabulary	Grammar
Welcome p. 6		Future with *will* • Future with *going to* • Present continuous with future aspect • Vocabulary review	
1 p. 10	Performing arts	• Music genres • Gradable and ungradable adjectives • Intensifiers	• Linking words (addition, contrast, opposition, conclusion, summary)
2 p. 22	Values	• Values • Noun suffixes	• Modals (*should*, *must*, *have to*, *can*—to talk about rules)
Review 1 p. 34 - **Review 2** p. 35			
3 p. 36	Taking a stand	• Expressions to give your opinion, to agree and to disagree with someone	• *Too*, *either*, *neither* • Modals (*may*, *might*, *could*—to talk about possibilities)
4 p. 48	Well-being	• Word formation (nouns and verbs) • Activities related to well-being	• Linking words (condition) • Zero conditional • First conditional
Review 3 p. 60 - **Review 4** p. 61			
5 p. 62	Visual arts	• Collocations (adjectives + preposition)	• Second conditional
6 p. 74	Consumerism	• Appliances and gadgets • Chores	• Present perfect • *Yet*, *already*, *for*, *since*
Review 5 p. 86 - **Review 6** p. 87			
7 p. 88	Conflict resolution	• Verbs to describe how to handle conflicts	• Present perfect vs. simple past • Tag questions
8 p. 100	Creativity	• *Make* vs. *do* • Collocations with the word *creativity*	• Review
Review 7 p. 112 - **Review 8** p. 113			

Makerspace p. 114 **Language Reference** p. 118 **Branch Out** p. 130 **Glossary** p. 132

	Listening	Speaking	Reading	Writing	Pronunciation
	• Talent show commentary	• Talent show commentary	• Letter to the editor	• Letter to the editor	• Weak and strong forms of *and* and *but*
	• Discussion	• Discussion	• Instructional texts	• Instructional text	• /ɾ/
	• Speech	• Speech	• Journalistic argumentative text	• Argumentative text	• Heteronyms
	• Debate	• Debate	• Infographic	• Short infographic	• Catenation
	• Audioguide	• Audioguide	• Online forum	• Online forum	• /ʌ/ vs. /ʊ/
	• Podcast	• Presentation	• Ad	• Ad	• Syllable division
	• Discussion with a mediator	• Discussion with a mediator	• Photo-essay	• Photo-essay	• Intonation in tag questions
	• Opinion	• Opinion	• Meme	• Meme	• Commonly mispronounced words

FIG. 1
CINDERELLA
DRACULA
BRAM STOKER
BRAVE NEW WORLD
ALDOUS HUXLEY
STOP

WELCOME

1 Look at pages 6 and 7 and list the elements in the image that refer to your daily routine. Then talk to a classmate and say how these elements are part of your life.

Cellphone, books, television.

2 Choose two items from your list and write a sentence about how each of them might impact on your life in the future.

In the future, I think I won't read printed books, only e-books. I think I won't watch on Television anymore and the cellphone will be very important

3 Match each of the excerpts from online news to its corresponding section. Not every section will be used.

1 Experts say the diet of 2050 will revolve less around meat and more around bugs.

2 Every medical malady will be treatable with a miracle pill.

3 The world will end on both April 23 and June 24 in a double whammy of apocalypses, some theorists claim.

4 Our fridge will let shopping websites know we are out of milk and it will be delivered by a drone.

a [ ] Politics
b [2] Health
c [ ] Style
d [4] Technology
e [3] Entertainment
f [ ] Sports
g [1] Food
h [2] Science

4 All the pieces of news mentioned in activity 3...

a [1] introduce some evidence for a fact that is presented.
b [4] mention timetabled future events.
c [3] show predictions about the future.
d [2] present future arrangements.

5 Read the news excerpts in activity 3 again. Do you agree with their predictions? Why?

6 Look at the images and write news headlines for each of them. Share your ideas with a classmate.

1

Health programation

2

Street

3

Pill instead of a meal

4

7 Choose one of the images on pages 6 and 7 and write your own headline about the future. Share your ideas on #MAKERS Digital <www.richmondmakers.com>. Use the hashtag #ViewingTheFuture.

____

8 Use the words and expressions from the box to complete the post. Not all of them will be used.

appreciating	as	can't stand
don't mind	enough	going to
looking	the most	who / will

Alicia Marshall

Have you ever imagined what life (1) _______ be like a hundred years from now?

A number of technology forecasters have theorized about the future, but in fact not much has been discussed about how we can profit (or not) from what is predicted in such visionary insights.

If you (2) _______ having your food prepared for you by digital devices, you may like to know that a 3-D printer can provide you with your favorite dishes in one click, since you will be able to download and print ready-to-eat food in minutes. But if you are the kind of person (3) _______ takes pleasure in cooking, smelling and tasting your own culinary creations, that experience might not be interesting (4) _______. (5) _______ works of art, watching a play and meeting people have already become a matter of using your devices, so no wonder experiences won't be (6) _______ intense as they used to be before technology took over our lives. What do you think about it?

Add story · Edit profile · More · + Add more details · + Add to highlights · About · Photos · Friends

Like · Comment · Share

9 Do you agree with the post? Do you think it presents a positive view of the future?

10 Write a comment reacting to the post in activity 8. Then discuss your comment with a classmate.

____

____

____

____

____

____

____

11 Complete the sentences with the correct future tense of the verbs in parentheses.

1 Our project aims at helping the environment, so we _______ (plant) a tree.

2 _______ you _______ (bake) a cake for John's birthday? He has been quite anxious about it.

3 Our coworkers _______ (meet) us next Monday.

4 Robots _______ (replace) the human workforce completely in the next few years.

5 I _______ (look) for a new apartment because mine has to be refurbished.

6 I _______ (read) more books next semester.

12 Complete the sentences so that they are true for you.

1 I avoid _______________.

2 Most of my friends prefer _______________.

3 I'm considering _______________.

4 My family and I are planning to _______________.

13 Find and correct the mistake in each sentence.

1 Nobody isn't going to sleep in my class.

____

2 Is anything ready for some adventure?

____

3 Everything can do it. It's so easy!

____

4 She ate anything that was in the bowl. She was really hungry!

____

14 Circle the correct options to complete the leaflet.

Have you ever felt like you have more to offer but don't know what to do? Are you enthusiastic (1) **enough** / **more** to play with our KIDS?

Register with #TeenHelpsKids and you will have the (2) **as** / **most** gratifying experience of your life!

Come and spend some time with our kids!

Visit our website for further information about our volunteering program.

1

IN THE LIMELIGHT

OBJECTIVES

- Discuss types of performing arts and how people relate to them.
- Comment and give opinions about performing arts.
- Talk about and stress the qualities of something.
- Connect ideas in a text in a meaningful way.
- Reflect on your involvement with performing arts.
- Write about your opinion on an article you've read.
- Reflect on the experience of going to the theater.
- Discuss the connection between dance and culture.

Read the questions and discuss.

1. Which form of art do you prefer: theater, dance or music?
2. Do you prefer to perform them or to watch other people performing them?
3. Would you like to perform any of them on a stage?
4. How important do you think these types of art are in people's lives?

Richmond

#MAKERS DIGITAL

1

2

3

4

5

RTV

1 **Look at the images on page 12 and match them to the types of art below.**

a ☐ musical
b ☐ breakdancing
c ☐ garage band
d ☐ alternative theater
e ☐ ballroom dancing

2 **Watch a video about an experiment done by Benjamin, Nathan, Neil and Luke. Then answer the questions.**

1 What is different about the kind of art they are producing?

___

2 Did the audience like the result?

___

3 **Watch the video again and order the steps of the production.**

a ☐ The production goes on stage.
b ☐ Benjamin and Nathan decide what the story is going to be about.
c ☐ Computers create lyrics.
d ☐ Computers analyze data and define what makes a good story.
e ☐ Computers write the music.

4 **Which of the images on page 12 best illustrates the work done by Benjamin, Nathan, Neil and Luke? Why?**

___

5 **Discuss with a classmate.**

1 Which types of art presented on page 12 do you prefer? Why?
2 Would you like to do any of them for fun or professionally?
3 Can computer-generated art be considered art? Why?
4 In your opinion, can the form of art represented in the other images also be created by a computer?

React!

6 **Write a comment about the video.**

JasperJ This is different from any kind of art I have ever seen.
48 min — 2 Great! Report

MusicalDora I wonder if I could use computers to write the lyrics for my band as well. This is the most difficult part for me!
37 min — 6 Great! Report

Omistra What's the name of this musical? Is it still on? I want to watch it!
25 min — 1 Great! Report

CandidRose Really? I don't think that actually works. Computers can't create real art!
12 min — 1 Great! Report

___

___

POST

I Wonder

7 **Write a question about popular theater productions in different countries. Then look for the answer.**

___

___

99 Great! 99 Interact

LANGUAGE 1

1 **Marisa and Jen went to a concert together and now they are telling their friend Julia about it. Read their dialogue and answer the questions.**

Julia: Did you go to the concert? How was it?

Marisa: Believe it or not, it was very bad.

Julia: Oh no!

Jen: Yeah, it was awful.

1 Do Marisa and Jen have similar opinions? ________

2 What is the meaning of "awful"? ________

3 Which word is used to intensify the meaning of the adjective "bad"? ________

2 **Use the adjectives in the box to complete the chart.**

amazing	captivating	funny	sad
~~awful~~	depressing	good	stunning
~~bad~~	fabulous	hilarious	terrible
beautiful	fantastic	interesting	terrific

Gradable adjectives	Ungradable adjectives
bad	awful

3 **Write a gradable adjective from activity 2 next to the corresponding ungradable adjective in the list below.**

1 awful bad
2 amazing ________
3 fantastic ________
4 hilarious ________
5 depressing ________
6 stunning ________
7 terrible ________
8 terrific ________
9 fabulous ________
10 captivating ________

4 **Last weekend there was a cultural festival in town with different attractions, and now a group of friends is talking about what they did there. Complete their conversation with ungradable adjectives from activity 2. Make sure you don't repeat any of them.**

Laura: Hi, guys! How was your weekend? Did you see anything good at the festival?

Anthony: I did! I went to an (1) ________ play, the actors were really talented!

Marie: And I saw a ballet presentation! It was (2) ________! The music was perfect, and the scenography and costumes were (3) ________. How about you?

Laura: Oh, I went to a stand-up comedy act. It was (4) ________! And I went to a concert too! It was absolutely (5) ________! It's definitely in my top 3 best concerts.

Josh: You guys are so lucky! I watched a movie and it was (6) ________. I'm pretty sure it's the worst film I've ever seen.

5 **Check the intensifiers that can be used with ungradable adjectives.**

1 ☐ very
2 ☐ really
3 ☐ absolutely
4 ☐ completely
5 ☐ extremely
6 ☐ exceptionally
7 ☐ particularly
8 ☐ totally

Study Space My Glossary

6 **Read the different kinds of concerts that usually take place at cultural festivals. Then use the intensifiers and adjectives of the previous activities to write your opinion on each of them.**

1 Pop music is ________.
2 Rock music is ________.
3 EDM is ________.
4 Classical music is ________.
5 Rap is ________.
6 Reggaeton is ________.
7 Country music is ________.
8 Hip-hop is ________.

LISTENING AND SPEAKING

1 Look at the images and discuss the questions in pairs.

1 What kind of TV shows are these?

2 What do you know about them?

3 Do you like this kind of TV show? Why?

2 2 **Listen to the comments the coaches made in four auditions. Then check the singers who were selected for the next phase of the program.**

1 ☐ Rwanda Shaw

2 ☐ Suzanne Gay

3 ☐ Hollywood Anderson

4 ☐ Cassadee Pope

3 3 **Listen again and pay attention to the coaches' comments. Then refer to the numbers in activity 2 to match the comments to the corresponding singer.**

a ☐ "Even if you had started right, it would still have been wrong."

b ☐ "You do really come across really cool, really comfortable on stage."

c ☐ "I just wanna hear you singing."

d ☐ "You've got an awesome voice."

e ☐ "That was beautiful."

f ☐ "You've got so much potential."

Buzzwords

***"I'm so hype** right now."*

What does "I'm so hype" mean? Look it up!

Study Space

Makerspace p. 114

4 **Are the coaches' comments below positive, negative or descriptive?**

1 "Other than the lyrics, it wasn't remotely like Whitney Houston." ________

2 "I think there is more to the problem than you starting off wrong." ________

3 "That was so well executed." ________

4 "You had something a little country in there." ________

5 **Consider the comments in activity 4 to answer the questions below.**

1 Which negative comment is more tactful?

2 How can we make the blunt comment more tactful?

3 How does the singer react to the negative comment?

Pronunciation

6 4 **How do we pronounce the words *but* and *and*? Listen and repeat.**

7 5 **Now listen to the same words in context. Are they pronounced in the same way? Explain.**

"You might have reacted physically, because it was great to see that, **but** you didn't falter."

"There's nobody else like you **and** I believe with 200% of my heart that you, Cassadee, are a superstar."

8 6 **Listen to the sentences below and identify whether the words *but* and *and* are being pronounced in a weak (W) or strong (S) form.**

1 ☐ He studied hard, but he failed the test.

2 ☐ In musicals, actors have to sing, act and dance well.

3 ☐ She tried hard, but the coaches didn't like her.

4 ☐ He can play the piano and sing.

9 **Is there a reason for using the strong form when the words *and* and *but* are in context? If so, which one? Can you think of similar examples?**

10 **Now practice saying the sentences from activity 8 with *and* and *but* both in their strong and weak forms.**

11 **Look for a famous singer's performance on video on the internet. What's your opinion about his/her performance? Remember to be tactful.**

12 **Share your opinion with a classmate and ask for his/her opinion on what you wrote. Make any necessary adjustments.**

13 **Record your opinion and share it on #MAKERS Digital <www.richmondmakers.com>. Use the hashtag #SingingContest.**

READING

Before Reading

1 Scan the texts and check the correct answers to the questions.

1 What elements can you find in this kind of text?

a ☐ author's name
b ☐ a greeting
c ☐ reference to an article
d ☐ address
e ☐ signature
f ☐ title
g ☐ personal opinion
h ☐ informal text

2 Where can we find such elements?

a ☐ a letter to the editor
b ☐ a blog post
c ☐ a message to a friend

3 Where can you find this kind of text?

a ☐ magazines
b ☐ newspapers
c ☐ books
d ☐ internet

4 What do you think are good reasons to write this kind of text?

a ☐ Correct some information that appeared in the article.
b ☐ Complement the information presented in the article.
c ☐ Congratulate the author of the article for his/her text.
d ☐ Offer support to people in the situation described in the article.
e ☐ Express your opinion about the topic of the article.
f ☐ Express agreement or disagreement with the author of the article.

http://www.teenink.com

Makers' Talk

LOGIN | SIGN UP

HOME | ENTERTAINMENT | LIFESTYLE & WELLNESS | HOT TOPICS | CONTACT US

"Dancing in the air"
By Giovanni_D, Phx, Arizona

I found Dany Nagle's article "Dancing in the air" moving, and I can also relate to the joys of dancing. I can relate because Dany talks about how dancing makes her feel ("And when I nail a new move, I'm on top of the world…"). I feel the same way about my dancing. I don't dance for others. On the contrary, I dance for myself because, in the end, why else would I keep doing it? Besides, she talks about her passion for dancing and how nothing else matters when you dance, everything else disappears and no worries or problems in life can take that moment of dancing away. There are almost no words that can describe the feeling I have when I dance. It's the best! For Dany, true passion is all the motivation she needs, and this is true for me too. In brief, that is how I can relate to her article.

Adapted from <http://www.teenink.com/hot_topics/letters_to_the_editor/article/732245/Dancing-in-the-air/>. Accessed on July 26, 2018.

"Keeping Music Real"
By Maggie Vinton, No. Platte, NE

I agree with Abby H.'s article "Keeping Music Real". Music today is bland and offensive, with a strong emphasis on pop and rap. Our local radio station often plays the same song three times in only one hour! Usually it is a generic, ugly song that proves people are willing to settle for less. Moreover, Abby says that most songs fit into a slim mold, and I agree. Do we really need another song about how rich someone is? If that person is so rich, why do they need to make another repulsive song?
I don't like the newest artist or the latest American Idol. Therefore, most of my friends think I don't like any music. I wish others would give indie or alternative bands like The White Stripes or Franz Ferdinand a try. Sometimes, as Abby suggested, digging into your parents' old records can really pay off. However, I just hope people can realize there's more music in the world than bubblegum pop.

Adapted from <http://www.teenink.com/hot_topics/letters_to_the_editor/article/18011/Keeping-Music-Real/>. Accessed on July 21, 2018.

While Reading

2 **Read the letters to the editor on page 16 and answer: which of the reasons mentioned in item 4 of activity 1 have motivated Giovanni and Maggie to write them?**

____

____

3 **Write G (Giovanni), M (Maggie) or B (both) to identify who mentions the items below.**

1 [ ] the name of the article
2 [ ] quotes from the article
3 [ ] the most important information from the article
4 [ ] opinion about the original article or its topic
5 [ ] examples of artists they like
6 [ ] examples of artists they don't like
7 [ ] personal examples or factual evidence

4 **Which of the items in activity 3 are essential in a message to the editor of a magazine or website?**

____

____

____

5 **Look back at the letters and underline, in both of them, examples of the essential items you mentioned in activity 4.**

6 **Read the letters again and answer the questions.**

1 Why does Giovanni relate to the article he read?

____

2 Why does Giovanni dance?

____

3 Is it easy for Giovanni to describe what he feels when he dances?

____

4 What does Maggie say about the local radio stations?

____

5 Why do most of Maggie's friends think she doesn't like music?

____

6 What kind of bands does Maggie like?

____

7 **Match the expressions below to their definition.**

1 to nail something
2 to be on top of the world
3 nothing else matters
4 to be bland
5 to settle for something
6 bubblegum

a [ ] to be very happy
b [ ] to accept or agree to something
c [ ] everything else is unimportant
d [ ] simplistic, superficial
e [ ] to be uninteresting or boring
f [ ] to perform something successfully

8 **Find the expressions from activity 7 in the letters. Then use them to write about Giovanni's and Maggie's opinions.**

1 Giovanni

____

____

2 Maggie

____

____

After Reading

9 **How do you feel about dancing and music? Do you agree with Giovanni and Maggie? Choose at least two expressions from activity 7 to write your opinion on these topics.**

1 ______________________________

2 ______________________________

10 **Discuss these questions in pairs.**

1 What do you do when you read an article and you really like it or completely disagree with the author?
2 Have you ever written a message to someone reacting to an article you read?
3 What would motivate you to write to the editor of a magazine or website commenting on an article you read?

Study Space

Workbook p. 137

LANGUAGE 2

1 **The sentences below were extracted from the letters to the editor on page 16. Read and circle the best options to complete the statements about them.**

"**On the contrary**, I dance for myself..."

"**Besides**, she talks about her passion for dancing..."

"**In brief**, that is how I can relate to her article."

"**Moreover**, Abby says that most songs fit into a slim mold..."

"**Therefore**, most of my friends think I don't like any music."

"**However**, I just hope people can realize there's more music in the world than bubblegum pop."

1. These words are used to **compare** / **connect** ideas.
2. Their use implies that **everything** / **something** has been said about the topic.
3. These words **can** / **can't** be removed from these sentences.
4. If we remove these words from the sentences, **there is no impact on the text** / **the relation between the ideas is not clear**.

Linking Words

Linking words are words and phrases that connect sentences. They may contrast ideas and information, provide additional information, explain cause and effect, provide reasons, make comparisons and conclude arguments. Examples:

- I like going to concerts **and** to the theater.
- She said she's going, **so** I believe her.
- He would like to watch the play, **but** it is too expensive.
- **Although** they are tired, they continue working.
- He doesn't think it will be much fun. **On the other hand**, he has never done anything like that before.
- **In summary**, that's what I understood from the article.

2 **Read the examples below. Then write the words in bold from activity 1 in the correct column according to the idea they convey.**

Addition	Conclusion	Contrast	Opposition	Summarizing
and	so	although but	on the contrary	in summary

3 **Fabio has just had his letter published by the *Makers' Talk* magazine. Underline the correct options to complete his dialogue with Ian.**

Fabio: I can't believe it! The e-mail that I wrote to *Makers' Talk* was published!

Ian: Why did you write to them?

Fabio: (1) **However**, / **Although** many people think this is silly, I really think we have to share our opinions.

Ian: I don't think this is silly. (2) **On the contrary**, / **So** I believe that this is the best way for them to know their readers' opinions. (3) **Besides that**, / **In brief**, I have already sent them some messages myself. I was just surprised because I didn't know you read this magazine.

Fabio: You're right. I usually don't read it. (4) **However**, / **Although** Samantha sent me the link for an interesting article about a boy who was bullied at school. His only friend left school, so he had to find a way to make new friends. That's when he joined a band.

Ian: (5) **Besides that**, / **In brief**, his story is similar to yours, right?

Fabio: Exactly.

4 **Match the sentences below. Pay attention to the linking words used and the idea they convey.**

1. Although the actors are extremely talented, ...
2. Anna, my best friend, is a great singer and an excellent composer.
3. John has performed in public many times and with great artists.
4. Monica told everybody that she didn't like the show.

a [ ] Moreover, she plays the drums very well.

b [ ] the performance was not very good.

c [ ] However, I saw her having lots of fun with her friends in the crowd.

d [ ] Besides that, he has been studying classical ballet for a long time.

5 **Rewrite the sentences from activity 4 inverting the clauses.**

1. Although the performance was not very good, the actors are extremely talented.
2.
3.
4.

6 Complete the conversations with the linking words from the box.

besides that | however | in brief | on the contrary | so

1 **A:** Did you like Mary's performance in the school's talent show?

B: She sang a very beautiful song. __________, I think she needed to tune her guitar.

2 **A:** What do you think of Ed Sheeran?

B: His voice is beautiful, he plays the guitar very well and his songs are nice. __________, he's a perfect artist!

3 **A:** I heard that the audience did not like John's performance. Is that true?

B: The audience did not like his performance?! __________, they loved it!

4 **A:** Why should I go to the theater with you?

B: Because the play is so moving and inspiring! __________, the cast is fantastic!

5 **A:** I know we have already talked about this, but what did you think about the play you watched last week?

B: Well, the story is very good and flows naturally, __________ time flies when you watch it.

7 Connect the sentences below using the prompts in parentheses.

1 John decided to play a new musical instrument. We cannot afford one now.

(however) John decided to play a new musical instrument. However, we cannot afford one now.

2 Kyle is great at dancing, singing and acting. He is a great artist.

(in brief) ______________________________

____

3 Janet hasn't been rehearsing her lines. The director is probably going to be angry.

(therefore) ______________________________

____

4 Phil and Gina haven't missed any dance classes. They were always early and even helped the teacher prepare the classroom.

(on the contrary) ______________________________

____

8 Can you replace the linking words in activity 7 by others with the same meaning? Think and rewrite the sentences.

1 ______________________________

____

2 ______________________________

____

3 ______________________________

____

4 ______________________________

____

9 Look at the images and complete the sentences according to them.

1

She thought the ballet move was easy. However, __________.

2

Many people thought the concert would be a failure. On the contrary, __________.

3

He forgot to study his lines and didn't rehearse with the rest of the actors. Therefore, __________.

4

Although __________, they loved their performance.

Study Space   Workbook p. 137

WRITING

Writing a Letter to the Editor

Before Writing

A WORD ON ARTISTIC POLITICAL CORRECTNESS

By Esther Davis

It is very safe to say that imagination has no limits; therefore, it is also possible to say that art has no limits, since it is a fruit of humans' imagination. That may be so, but nowadays the concept of limitless art is under attack. Every film, song or book that hits the limelight is scrutinized through a new lens: the cultural appropriation perspective.

Cultural appropriation can be defined as "the unacknowledged or inappropriate adoption of the practices, ideas, customs etc. of one society or people by members of another and more dominant one". It can take many forms, from a Caucasian actor playing a Japanese *manga* character in a film, to a singer wearing a *saree*, a traditional Indian dress in a music video that is clearly not Indian.

It is a delicate matter and it should always be taken into consideration by artists, but, in many ways, it also limits imagination. So, the big question here is: how do we balance or even differentiate cultural appropriation from cultural appreciation?

Based on <http://www.theweek.co.uk/cultural-appropriation>. Accessed on July 30, 2018.

1 **Plan your letter to the editor about the article "A Word on Artistic Political Correctness". Think about the following:**

- your opinion of the article;
- your motivation to write to the editor;
- what you want to express: your opinion of the article, the topic of the article or both;
- personal example or factual evidence to support your opinion;
- which pieces of information from the article you are going to include in your letter.

Drafting

2 **Write a draft of your letter.**

3 **Share your letter with a classmate and ask for his/her opinion. Make adjustments, if necessary.**

Final Writing

4 **Write the final version of your letter. Share it on #MAKERS Digital <www.richmondmakers.com>. Use the hashtag #LetterToTheEditor.**

INVESTIGATE

I watch ____________ plays, concerts, movies or dance performances in a month.

Collect Data

- Throughout the month, keep a record of all theater plays, music concerts, movies and dance performances you watch—either in person, on TV, online etc.
- Follow your teacher's instructions to make a chart in your notebook to register the data. In the "Record of productions" column, make a tally mark for each cultural production you watch.
- At the end of the month, add up all the tally marks related to each of the cultural productions and write the total number in the last column. This way, you will find out the exact number of plays, concerts, movies and dance performances you have seen.
- Then add up all the final numbers to find out how many cultural productions you have watched in a month.

Analyze the Data

- How many plays/concerts/movies/dance performances did you watch?
- Which kind of artistic performance was more frequently watched this month?
- Do you think the number of performance you watch in different months would be similar?
- How do your results compare with the ones of your classmates?

Draw a Conclusion

I watch ____________ plays, concerts, movies or dance performances in a month.

1 **Reflect on your conclusions and discuss.**

1. Are you more or less involved with artistic performances than you expected?
2. Would you like to watch more cultural productions as part of your routine? Which ones?
3. Do you think that artistic performances are important?

2 **Share your ideas on #MAKERS Digital <www.richmondmakers.com>. Use the hashtag #PerformingArtsAndMe.**

LOCAL AND GLOBAL

1 **Look at the images and discuss the questions with a classmate.**

a

b

c

d

1 Do you know these dances?
2 Where are they from?
3 Do you know anything else about them? What?

2 **Reflect, research and take notes on your findings.**

1 What is the connection between these dances and the culture of their country of origin?
2 Are there any special conditions for them to be performed? Can they be performed anywhere, anytime and by anyone?
3 Can you learn how to dance them in your country?
4 What are the typical dances from your country? Are they also known and practiced in other countries?

3 **Organize a field trip to watch a typical dance performance with your classmates.**

IMAGINE

Imagine going to the theater and not seeing the play.

1 **Research into the concept. Bring your research to be discussed in class.**

2 **Read the magazine article. Then discuss the questions with a classmate.**

1 What is the most important thing in a play?
2 Is sight important to experience the theater?
3 How do you think you would feel "watching" a similar play?

RTV

2

REAL VALUES

OBJECTIVES

- Discuss the concept of values and their importance.
- Talk about different values.
- Reflect on why people may have different values in life.
- Talk about different cultures and how their beliefs and habits may vary.
- Describe social rules in different contexts.
- Reflect on following one's own values.
- Develop awareness about stereotypes and cultural generalizations.

Read the questions and discuss.

1. How would you define "values"?
2. In your opinion, are values always good?
3. How do you think people's beliefs influence their behavior?
4. How can people's values influence their achievements in life?

Richmond
#MAKERS
DIGITAL
1
2
3
4
5

RTV

1 **The images on page 24 show moments of personal achievement. Look at them and answer the questions.**

1 What motivates people to face challenges?

2 What values do people show when they do it?

3 Which challenges are the people in the images dealing with? Why?

4 Which of these activities would be a challenge for you? Why?

5 How do you deal with your own challenges?

2 **Watch the video of Shona dealing with something she is scared of and answer the questions.**

1 What is Shona scared of? ____________________

2 Why is she scared? ____________________

3 When did Shona last ride a horse? ____________________

4 What is she doing to deal with her fear? ____________________

3 **Watch the video again and correct the sentences.**

1 Shona doesn't have her own horse.

____

2 Shona's mother is afraid for her.

____

3 In the end, Shona gives up riding.

____

4 **In your opinion, is Shona's story inspiring? Why?**

____

5 **What values does Shona show in the video?**

____

React!

6 **Write your own comment about the video.**

BenKin2005 Shona's really cool! Riding horses like that is crazy! She has a lot of discipline and determination for sure.

2 days ago

JillJOJO I used to be afraid of the sea, but I decided to learn how to swim! I'm crazy about it now! Congratulations, Shona!!! Commitment and optimism all the way!

5 days ago

ImJohnBrlk What a great story! It has inspired me to practice for my public speaking competition at school! #motivation

1 week ago

____

____

POST

I Wonder

7 **Write a question about how people usually overcome their fears. Then look for the answer.**

____

____

99 Great! 99 Interact

LANGUAGE 1

1 Match the columns to form values.

1	determin-	a	2	-ity
2	reliabil-	b	4	-ness
3	positi-	c	5	-ment
4	kind-	d	1	-ation
5	commit-	e	6	-ism
6	optim-	f	3	-vity

Snack Learning

All the words in activity 1 are **nouns**. Nouns can be used to identify a person, a place, a thing, an idea or a concept. You can create nouns by adding a suffix to another word (e.g.: a verb or an adjective). Some noun suffixes are:

- *-ance/ence:* perseverance, persistence
- *-ation*: information, motivation, preparation
- *-dom*: freedom, kingdom
- *-ism*: capitalism, optimism
- *-hood*: brotherhood, sisterhood, childhood
- *-ment*: government, commitment, disappointment
- *-ness*: kindness, happiness, usefulness

2 Choose the best noun to complete each definition.

compassion fairness loyalty perseverance reliability

1 Fairness is the quality of treating people equally.

2 Perseverance is the quality of having continued determination.

3 Compassion is a feeling of sympathy for someone who is suffering and a wish to help them.

4 Loyalty is the quality of being trustworthy.

5 Reliability is the quality of constantly being supportive.

Study Space

3 Which of the values in activity 2 do you think are more important for society? Why?

4 Do you think your community needs to strengthen any of these values? Which one(s)?

My Glossary

5 Check the best value to complete each sentence.

1 Without ______, people see no meaning in what they do.

- a [ ] kindness
- b [x] passion
- c [ ] information

2 ______ is the quality of always being true.

- a [ ] Readiness
- b [x] Honesty
- c [ ] Freedom

3 Without ______ and original thinking, things never change.

- a [x] open-mindedness
- b [ ] usefulness
- c [ ] disappointment

4 Most people in the past lived a life of ______, with few possessions and little money.

- a [ ] preparation
- b [ ] optimism
- c [x] simplicity

5 Good teachers should focus not only on ______, but also on students' well-being.

- a [ ] passion
- b [x] result orientation
- c [ ] fairness

6 Do you agree with the statements in activity 5? Talk to a classmate and change the sentences you do not agree with.

7 Josie is interviewing some teenagers for a school project. She wants to know the most important values for them. Write the values based on what each teenager says.

Name	Answer
Tabatha	The most important value for me is (1) honesty. Sometimes we lie to protect people, but we end up hurting them sooner or later.
	Another thing I really value is (2) Fairness. We should treat people equally, regardless of who they are or how much money they have.
Phillip	To me, the quality of being generous, friendly and considerate is what can really make the world a better place. I would define it as (3) Compassion
	(4) Perseverance, or the ability of being firm in purpose even though something seems difficult, is essential so that people achieve things.

8 7 Listen to the interviews and check your answers to activity 7.

9 Do you agree with the teenagers' opinions in activity 7? Why?

LISTENING AND SPEAKING

1 **Discuss the questions with a classmate.**

1 Read the definition of "values". Do you think it is a good definition?

values
Beliefs about what is right and wrong and what is important in life.

Available at <https://www.oxfordlearnersdictionaries.com/definition/english/value_1>. Accessed on February 8, 2019.

2 Are all values positive? Can a person have negative values?

3 Are we born with a set of values or do we choose our values as we grow up?

4 What influences our values the most?

2 8 **Listen to part of a talk show and answer the questions.**

1 How many different people talk during this part of the show? ________

2 Are the hosts of the show children, teenagers or adults? ________

3 What are they talking about? ________

3 9 **Listen to the talk show again. What do the participants say about values? Check the correct options.**

1 ☐ They are our guides.

2 ☐ We are born with them.

3 ☐ They are not fixed.

4 ☐ They come only from friends.

5 ☐ They initially come from our families.

6 ☐ They are a choice after some time.

7 ☐ They are the government's responsibility.

4 **Write *Yes* or *No*. Can we say that...**

1 according to the participants of the talk show, our behavior is independent of our values? ________

2 all the participants of the talk show agree that we are not born with a fixed set of values? ________

3 the mediator of the talk show does not express his opinion on the topic? ________

4 according to the mediator of the talk show, selfishness is a value? ________

5 all the teenagers on the talk show agree that family influences one's values? ________

Pronunciation

5 **Discuss the questions with a classmate.**

1 Where do you think the participants of the talk show are from?

2 How do you know that?

6 10 **Listen to the sentences. How are the words in bold pronounced differently by the participants of the talk show and by an American speaker?**

1 I **don't** think we're born with our own sets of values.

2 Let's open this up to the **audience**.

3 [...] it depends on where the person was **brought up**.

4 [...] you're not born with a fixed **set of** values.

7 **Do you know what a flap sound (/ɾ/) is? Do some research and find it out.**

8 **Underline where the flap sound could occur in the following sentences.**

1 Teddy, are you coming home?

2 This is a metal box.

3 Why don't you rest a little?

4 He sent me an audio file.

5 Let's talk about Angela.

9 11 **Listen to the sentences in activity 8 and check your answers. Then practice saying them.**

Study Space

10 **Do you agree with the participants of the talk show's views? Talk to a classmate and justify your answers.**

11 **In small groups, organize a short talk show. Discuss the role these instances play in our choice of values:**

- school;
- family;
- government;
- media;
- friends;
- ourselves.

12 **Record your talk show and share it on #MAKERS Digital <www.richmondmakers.com>. Use the hashtag #Values.**

READING

Before Reading

1. Would you like to visit any places whose culture is very different from yours? Which one(s)? Do you think their values are different from yours? Yes. Italy, France, India...

2. What type of preparations do we need to make before we visit a place whose culture is different from ours? Do you think it is important to research into this place's core values?
Researchs and planning the days with the activity. Sure.

3. Look at the texts. What type of information do you expect to find in them?

1

https://www.tripadvisor.com

Thailand: A Guide to Appropriate Behavior

Take off your shoes!

When entering a Thai home or temple, it is customary to remove your shoes. This is not simply a religious custom, but has practical cleanliness benefits too. Some homes, businesses and temples will provide indoor slippers for use only inside their buildings. You will probably see them just outside the main doorway. Alternatively, you can enter barefoot or wearing socks. However, try not to point your feet at anyone and keep them out of sight when sitting.

10 comments

Adapted from <https://www.tripadvisor.com/Travel-g293915-c88836/Thailand:A.Guide.To.Appropriate.Behaviour.html>. Accessed on August 7, 2018.

2

Travel Guide | Thailand

Don't lose face in Thailand!

As in many Asian cultures, the concept of face plays a large role in Thailand. Being confrontational, losing your temper or showing strong negative emotions in public are frowned upon in Thai culture. Not only will you lose face, you will also find that this sort of behavior is not productive in accomplishing what you want. Avoid doing anything that may embarrass yourself or your Thai friends. In short, you should try to keep a low profile.

Adapted from <https://www.reachtoteachrecruiting.com/guides/thailand/etiquette-in-thailand/>. Accessed on August 7, 2018.

3 TRIP TIPS

When in Thailand, eat up your rice!

In a typical Thai meal, there are several dishes at the center of the table and a plate of rice for every guest. You are supposed to help yourself with the spoon in the main dish, not with your personal spoon. It's better to help yourself small portions several times rather than a big portion. The fork is used to push the food into the spoon and the spoon is used to eat. You mustn't eat rice with your fork. There are no knives on the table—as Thai food is already minced, you have nothing to cut. Chopsticks are rarely used, especially for noodle soups. Last, but not least, because rice is difficult to grow and harvest, and because it is essential in Thailand, it is considered disrespectful to leave it on the plate.

Adapted from <https://www.onlychaam.com/dos-and-donts-in-thailand/>. Accessed on August 7, 2018.

While Reading

4 **Read the texts on page 28 and check your answers to activity 3.**

5 **What type of texts are these? Circle the correct option.**

a Instructional. b Historical. c Narrative.

6 **Check the main characteristics of this type of text.**

a [ ] A title.

b [ ] Information about what people should and must do.

c [ ] Information about what people should not and cannot do.

d [ ] Information about what happened in the past.

e [ ] Complex and formal language.

f [ ] Verbs in the imperative form.

7 **What is the authors' intention with these texts? Circle the correct option.**

a Convince people not to go to Thailand.

b Promote Thailand as a travel destination.

c Criticize some of the Thai habits and customs.

d Create a discussion about cultural differences.

e Help people who want to travel to Thailand.

8 **Where can you usually find instructional texts?**

a [ ] Travel guides.

b [ ] Instruction manuals.

c [ ] Recipe books.

d [ ] Novels.

9 **Label each image with a word from the texts.**

10 **Correct the sentences according to the texts.**

1 You mustn't walk barefoot inside temples, homes and buildings.

2 Showing negative emotions in public is encouraged in Thailand.

3 In Thailand, people don't usually share food.

4 It is preferable to take a large portion of food on your plate.

11 **Answer the questions about Thai customs according to the texts.**

1 What shouldn't you do with your feet?

2 How should you use cutlery in Thailand?

3 Is it essential to use a knife when eating Thai food? Why?

4 What should you do with your rice? Why?

After Reading

12 **Discuss the questions with a classmate.**

1 Are any of the Thai customs similar to yours?

2 Are there any rules that should be followed when visiting your country?

Study Space

Buzzwords!

*Don't **lose face** in Thailand!*
What does the expression "lose face" mean? Look it up!

13 **Have you ever lost face? Tell a classmate about it.**

Workbook p. 139

LANGUAGE 2

1 Read the sentences and check the function of the words in bold.

Alternatively, you **can** enter barefoot or wearing socks.
In short, you **should** try to keep a low profile.
You **mustn't** eat rice with your fork.

They are being used to describe...

a [ ] intentions and expectations.
b [X] rules and suggestions.
c [ ] predictions and probability.

Modal Verbs

Modal verbs are auxiliary verbs, which means that they accompany the main verb in a sentence. They can be used to express ability, obligation, possibility and suggestion, among other ideas.

People **should** remove their shoes.
People **should not/shouldn't** show the sole of their feet.
Should people greet everyone the same way?
Yes, they **should**. / No, they **shouldn't**.

Attention!

Sometimes the negative form of a modal verb changes its meaning.

HAVE TO

You **have to** dress properly when you visit a temple. → obligation
You **don't have** to bring a gift when you visit someone. → It's not an obligation, but you can do it if you want to.

CAN

You **can** visit the temples. → possibility or permission
You **can't** wear shoes in the temples. → prohibition

2 Put the sentences under the correct category.

1 You **should** always give up your seat to the elderly.
2 You **can** call your friends by their first names.
3 You **must** respect everyone regardless of who they are.
4 You **have to** take a shower regularly.
5 You **can't** chew gum during class.
6 You **mustn't** use your smartphone during school tests.

Permission	Obligation	Suggestion	Prohibition
2	3, 4	1	5, 6

3 Which of the statements in activity 2 are false in your reality? Rewrite them to make them true for you. None of them.

4 Match the signs to the correct rules.

1

2

3

4

a [3] You should be careful when driving, there are wild animals in the area.
b [1] You can park your car here.
c [4] You mustn't stop your car here.
d [2] You can't bring your dog here.

5 Cross out the extra word in each sentence.

1 You should have tell your parents the truth about your test results.
2 People can to wake up later during vacations.
3 You do must always be kind to everyone around you.
4 When you are visiting a foreign country, you don't can't always do what you want.
5 You not should never assume people will speak English, so it's a good idea to learn a few basic words in the country's native language.

6 Underline the correct option to complete each sentence.

1 It's a hospital, you **don't have to** / **mustn't** smoke.
2 The teacher said we **can** / **must** read this book, but only if we want to.
3 If you want to learn how to speak English well, you **can't** / **must** work hard.
4 The entrance to the museum is free, but we **can** / **have to** leave a voluntary donation.
5 You **should** / **mustn't** carry your passport with you at all times when travelling.

7 Bill and Ron are talking about cultural differences. Complete their dialogue with a modal verb from the box and the verbs in parentheses.

can can't have to don't have to should shouldn't

Bill: Have you ever been to Germany, Ron?

Ron: Yes, I have. I lived there for a year.

Bill: That's great! I'm going there next month. Is there any cultural aspect I should pay attention to?

Ron: Well, I guess every culture has its peculiarities. German people tend to be straightforward, so you (1) ______ (get) offended if they skip casual conversation and go straight to the point.

Bill: That's good to know. What else?

Ron: They're usually very disciplined people and they will probably tell you when you do something wrong.

Bill: I guess I (2) ______ (pay) attention to their rules.

Ron: Definitely! Especially traffic rules. You (3) ______ (take) a look at traffic rules before you travel. For example, you (4) ______ (jaywalk). There is even a fine for people who do it.

Bill: Interesting. What about food?

Ron: Potatoes are very typical of German cuisine. But you (5) ______ (eat) them in all meals. You (6) ______ (find) pizza almost everywhere.

Bill: Thanks, Ron!

8 12 Listen to the dialogue and check your answers to activity 7. What's the most surprising piece of information for you?

Study Space

9 Complete the sentences with your own ideas.

1 When you're talking to someone older, you should ______.

2 If you want to be a healthy person, you can't ______.

3 In order to embrace your passions in life, you must ______.

4 People who value diversity mustn't ______.

5 If you want to be remembered as an honest person, you must ______

10 Compare your sentences in activity 9 to a classmate's. Are they similar? Do you agree with your classmate's sentences?

11 Complete the leaflet with modal verbs and get ready for a field trip.

TOP TIPS TO MAKE THE MOST OUT OF A FIELD TRIP

▷ Before you go on your field trip, you (1) ______ make a list of the material you'll need to take with you, so that you don't forget anything.

▷ You (2) ______ carry too much weight with you, but if you need to carry a large bag, make sure you distribute the weight evenly inside it.

▷ Also check what you (3) ______ take with you. Depending on where you're going, cell phones are not allowed, for example.

▷ During the field trip, you (4) ______ always ask questions to your teacher or to the guide. So, if you have a doubt, ask them!

▷ You (5) ______ always do what the teacher or the guide says. This is not just a simple recommendation. This is essential for the organization of the field trip and for your safety.

Based on <http://blog.montgomeryschool.org/preparing-your-child-for-a-field-trip>. Accessed on July 30, 2018.

12 Write two rules or recommendations related to places you know. Follow the example.

1 A restaurant in your country.

a You don't have to tip the waiters.

b You shouldn't put your feet on the table.

2 A park in your country.

a ______

b ______

3 A museum in your country.

a ______

b ______

4 A library in your country.

a ______

b ______

Workbook p. 139

WRITING

Instructional Text About My Country's Dos and Don'ts

Before Writing

1 Plan your instructional text.

1. Where is your text going to be published? On a blog, in a school newsletter etc.?
2. Who is going to read your text? Teenagers from your country, teenagers from other countries etc.?
3. Which aspects of your culture do people consider really important? Make a list.
4. Which of them are you going to focus on? Choose three.
5. Do you want to encourage people to visit your country? Do you want to sound alarming? What overall message do you want to convey?

Drafting

2 Write a draft of your text.

3 Show your production to a classmate and ask for his/her opinion. Make adjustments, if necessary.

Final Writing

4 Write the final version of your instructional text. Share it on #MAKERS Digital <www.richmondmakers.com>. Use the hashtag #VisitingMyCountry.

INVESTIGATE

I **follow** / **don't follow** my own values.

Collect Data

- In your notebook, list three of your values.
- Write a list of actions that reflect the values you chose.
- For a week, monitor your everyday actions to see if you really live by and honor your values.
- Record your information in a chart like the following.
- Check your chart every time you take one of the listed actions.

My Values	Actions that Reflect my Values	Actions I Took

Analyze the Data

- How many times have you checked the actions you listed?
- Was there evidence that you follow some values more than others?
- Were the actions you chose a good way to determine if you follow your values?
- How difficult was it to monitor your own actions?

Draw a Conclusion

I **follow** / **don't follow** my own values.

1 Reflect on your conclusions and discuss.

1. If you follow your own values, do you think other people notice that?
2. If you don't completely follow your own values, what actions can you take to make sure that you walk your talk?
3. How difficult will it be to implement these actions into your daily routine?

2 Share your ideas on #MAKERS Digital <www.richmondmakers.com>. Use the hashtag #WalkYourTalk.

LOCAL AND GLOBAL

1 **Discuss the questions with a classmate.**

1 How would you define a stereotype?

2 Which stereotypes do you know?

3 Do you think it is a problem to believe stereotypes? Why?

2 **Read the newspaper article and check if it corroborates your ideas in activity 1.**

www.richmond.com.br

Is there any truth to stereotypes?

Jared Garcia | July 30, 2018

According to the Merriam-Webster Dictionary, a stereotype is "a standardized mental picture that is held in common by members of a group and that represents an oversimplified opinion, prejudiced attitude or uncritical judgment". Being stereotyped is a common—and usually unpleasant—experience, especially because we all feel unique. But is there any truth to stereotypes? Two big experiments published in 2005 and 2007 showed that some personality traits are more common in some cultures than in others. This could be due to genetics, migration patterns or other factors. For example, people who are more open to new experiences tend not to adapt to life in isolated communities, so they usually migrate to more populated places. Environmental aspects are also important—people tend to be less extroverted and open in places where there is higher risk of disease infection.

However, the personality traits found in the studies do not necessarily match the stereotypes we hold about cultures. For instance, Americans are believed to be much more extroverted than English people. But in the 2005 study, English people scored higher in extroversion than Americans. And in the 2007 study, Americans scored just a little bit higher than the English.

The conclusion of the 2005 study was that stereotypes are "social constructions designed to serve specific societal purposes". In other words, understanding the complex global patchwork of personalities demands dedicated investigation, and we find it easier—and comforting—to just simplify matters.

Based on <https://www.merriam-webster.com/dictionary/stereotype>; <http://www.bbc.com/future/story/20170413-different-nationalities-really-have-different-personalities>. Accessed on July 30, 2018.

3 **According to the article, what is a stereotype?**

4 **What are some of the stereotypes associated with people from your country? Are they true for you?**

5 **Choose a nationality and carry out some research into it.**

1 What stereotypes are held about this nationality?

2 Is there any truth to the stereotypes about this nationality? Why?

6 **Make a video about your findings in activity 5. Share it on #MAKERS Digital <www.richmondmakers.com>. Use the hashtag #Stereotypes.**

IMAGINE

Imagine changing your values.

1 **Research into the concept. Bring your findings to be discussed in class.**

2 **Read the online magazine article. Then discuss the questions with a classmate.**

RTV

1 What was the study's main finding?

2 What are some of the changes that happen throughout time?

3 In your opinion, which of your values will change?

REVIEW 1

1 Sally went to a show last night and posted several comments about it on a social network. Read and order her posts.

a ☐ In brief, he told me that they were perfect! I trusted him and got more positive about the concert.

b ☐ On the contrary, it was a complete disaster!

c ☐ Last night I went to the concert of one of my favorite bands in a very beautiful stadium. Although the stadium isn't far from a subway station, it took me 30 minutes to arrive there because the streets were very crowded.

d ☐ However, when they started playing, it was terrible! I was really disappointed because the studio versions of their songs are much better and I expected the concert to be just as good.

e ☐ Besides that, I didn't find my best friend in the middle of the crowd and had to walk alone. When I arrived, I finally found him and we started talking about the band. He told me that he had seen their concert before, that they were great musicians, that the songs were fantastic, that the guitar solos were fascinating...

f ☐ So, if you have a favorite band and have never been to their concert, don't go with high expectations because they may let you down.

2 13 Listen to Sally's complete post and check your answers.

3 Do you agree with the piece of advice Sally gives in the last part? Why?

____

____

4 Read Sally's posts again and find examples of the following elements.

1 two contrasting ideas:

____

2 an additional idea:

____

3 an opposing idea:

____

4 a summary idea:

____

5 a conclusive idea:

____

5 Write sentences about images using the prompts and the words from the box.

amazing awful captivating fabulous
fantastic stunning terrible terrific

1

(however / very bad)

I was very excited for the play. However, the actors were terrible and the music was awful.

2

(in summary / very beautiful)

____

3

(besides that / very good)

____

4

(on the contrary / very interesting)

____

6 Add an intensifier to make the sentences from activity 5 even stronger.

absolutely completely exceptionally
particularly really totally

1 ______________________________

2 ______________________________

3 ______________________________

4 ______________________________

REVIEW 2

1 Match the actions to the values they reflect.

1 Being nice to people around you.

2 Not telling another person's secret to anyone.

3 Not giving up when a situation becomes difficult.

4 Always telling the truth.

5 Accepting and understanding new ideas.

a [ ] Perseverance.
b [ ] Open-mindedness.
c [ ] Kindness.
d [ ] Honesty.
e [ ] Reliability.

2 How do actions reflect values? Explain how people who have these values act. Follow the example.

1 Compassion: If you have compassion as a value, you listen to other people's problems and try to help.

2 Commitment: ___

3 Fairness: ___

4 Loyalty: ___

5 Respect: ___

3 Complete the blog post about a teenager's most important values. Use the words from the box.

courage humor open-mindedness
respect simplicity

www.richmond.com.br

Having values is important for everybody. However, which values you consider more important will vary a lot depending on who you are. These are the values I treasure the most:

(1) ___. Life is full of challenges, so I believe brave people are able to deal with them better.

Sense of (2) ___. We must learn to laugh at ourselves.

(3) ___. We should not be afraid of change.

(4) ___. I think we live better when we don't accumulate superfluous things.

(5) ___. Regardless of who other people are, we owe them that.

4 What about you? Which values are important for you? Why?

___

5 Complete the telephone conversation using *must*, *have to*, *mustn't* and *don't have to*.

Fiona: I'm so excited about my trip to Brazil next month! What advice can you give me about your country, Matheus?

Matheus: Well, first of all, you (1) ___ check if you need a visa! Some nationalities are required to apply for a visa before entering Brazil.

Fiona: No worries. I've already done that. But I'm more concerned about some of the habits and traditions. Do I (2) ___ kiss people on the cheek when I meet them, for example?

Matheus: Well, Brazil is a very friendly country. You (3) ___ kiss everyone you meet, but people do this quite a lot. You (4) ___ be surprised if people invite you to go to places or do things with them. Brazilians are very welcoming.

Fiona: Nice. I heard that I (5) ___ tip waiters all the time. Is that true? How do I know when I (6) ___ do it or not?

Matheus: Well, usually the tip is included in the check. But you can give the waiter some extra cash if you really like the service.

Fiona: Thanks for the tips! I'm so excited! I (7) ___ forget to pack my sunscreen, though. It seems the weather will be fabulous!

6 Rewrite the social rules and recommendations using modal verbs. Follow the example.

1 You are prohibited to have pillow fights.
You mustn't have pillow fights.

2 It's only OK to make noise from Monday to Saturday.
___

3 It's not recommended to blow your nose in public.
___

4 You are obliged to let a chimney cleaner enter your house anytime.
___

5 Pedestrians are forbidden to walk in bicycle lanes.
___

7 Complete the sentence about the rules and recommendations in activity 6.

I think these rules and recommendations are from ___.

3

TAKE A STAND

OBJECTIVES

- Express opinions, agree and disagree politely.
- Identify the characteristics of an opinion article and understand its purpose.
- Infer information from a text.
- Write an opinion article.
- Investigate the current protests in your country.
- Identify fake news and check facts responsibly.
- Reflect on the importance of having and expressing opinions.

Read the questions and discuss.

1 Is it important to take a stand?

2 How important is it to give your opinion?

3 What are the relevant issues that people are fighting for nowadays?

4 What would you fight to change?

Richmond

#MAKERS DIGITAL

HeForShe
UN Women Solidarity Movement for Gender Equality

If not me, who?
If not now, when?

Emma Watson

RTV

1 **Look at the images on page 38. How are they connected? Discuss with a classmate.**

2 **Look at the images again and discuss the questions with a classmate.**

1 What is the campaign called?
2 What is it about?
3 Which organization promotes this campaign?
4 Why do you think the campaign was given this name?
5 What does Emma Watson mean with her quote?
6 Are you a HeForShe? Why?

3 14 **Listen to part of Emma Watson's speech at a UN conference in 2014. Then number the topics in the order they are mentioned.**

a ☐ gender not being two sets of opposing ideals
b ☐ Hillary Clinton's speech about women's rights
c ☐ how gender inequality affects men
d ☐ gender equality as an issue for both men and women

4 15 **Listen again and discuss the questions in pairs.**

1 Emma mentioned that less than 30% of Hillary Clinton's audience were male. Why did that stand out for her?
2 Why did she say "Men, I would like to take this opportunity to extend your formal invitation"? Why did people applaud?

5 **Do you agree with Emma's opinion that both men and women should participate in gender equality discussions? Why?**

React!

6 **Write a comment about Emma Watson's speech.**

IanGarcia I'd never realized the consequences of gender inequality for men. Very eye-opening speech!
2 days ago

Matilda Smith I don't know… Doesn't she give too much importance to men in her speech?
5 days ago

Georgina_Wats What an eloquent speech! Now guys have to sleep on it and decide where they stand.
1 week ago

____
____

Buzzwords

"Now guys have to ***sleep on it*** *and decide where they stand."*
What does "sleep on it" mean in this context? Look it up!

I Wonder

7 **Write a question about gender inequality in different countries. Then look for the answer.**

____
____

99 Great! 99 Interact

LANGUAGE 1

1 🎧16 **Listen to two young people talking about Emma Watson's speech. Identify if the expressions below are being used to present an opinion (O), to agree with something (A) or to disagree with something (D).**

1 ☐ As far as I'm concerned...
2 ☐ Fair enough.
3 ☐ I have a completely different opinion on that.
4 ☐ I have no doubt that...
5 ☐ I understand where you're coming from, but...
6 ☐ In my opinion...
7 ☐ That's a fair point, but...
8 ☐ I dare say...
9 ☐ I see what you're saying, but...
10 ☐ I agree with you...
11 ☐ I'm sure...

2 **Read some sentences from the conversation and match each expression in bold to another one that has the same meaning.**

1 **As far as I'm concerned**, men suffer the consequences of gender inequality much less than women.

2 **I have no doubt that** men should be included in the discussion.

3 **In my opinion**, everyone knows the problems women face as a consequence of gender inequality.

4 **I dare say that** not everyone realizes how we women suffer from gender inequality in our everyday lives!

5 **I'm certain that**, since she is such a well-known figure, she will reach many more people around the world.

6 Yes, **I agree with you** on that!

a ☐ from my point of view
b ☐ I am certain that
c ☐ I have a feeling that
d ☐ I share your views
e ☐ it goes without saying that
f ☐ it seems to me that

3 **The sentences below represent impolite ways to disagree with someone. Rewrite them using the expressions from activities 1 and 2.**

1 "No way! You are wrong about that!"

____

2 "Some things you say may be OK, but I don't agree with you."

____

3 "Are you crazy? You are completely wrong about this!"

____

4 "What you are saying is not totally wrong, but I have a different opinion."

____

Study Space   My Glossary

4 **Read the sentences and write a comment agreeing, disagreeing or expressing your opinion about them.**

1 Voting shouldn't be compulsory.

____

2 Global warming isn't as bad as people say it is.

____

3 Feminism is an issue that concerns only women.

____

4 There is no such thing as racism anymore.

____

5 There should be stricter laws against animal cruelty.

____

5 **Discuss your opinions from activity 4 with two classmates.**

LISTENING AND SPEAKING

1 17 **Listen to excerpts from three different speeches and check the correct options.**

1

Emma Gonzalez (activist)

In this part of her speech, Emma Gonzalez...

a ☐ defends her point of view by exposing facts.

b ☐ describes the feelings and the scene on the day of the shooting in her school.

c ☐ confronts people with different opinions from hers.

2

Viola Davis (actress)

We can infer that Viola Davis thinks...

a ☐ people are daydreaming.

b ☐ we need to keep creating laws.

c ☐ progress is achieved when everyone is included.

3

Martin Luther King, Jr. (minister and activist)

In his speech, Martin Luther King, Jr. doesn't imply that he wants...

a ☐ to end segregation in the United States.

b ☐ equal rights for African-American people.

c ☐ people to believe in their dreams.

2 18 **Listen to the speeches again and answer the questions.**

1 In Emma Gonzalez's speech, what do the numbers 17 and 15 refer to?

____

2 Why does Emma say everyone was altered after a little over 6 minutes?

____

3 What laws does Viola Davis mention in her speech?

____

4 Were these laws beneficial to people's lives?

____

5 What was Martin Luther King, Jr. fighting for?

____

6 Why did he mention the states of Georgia and Mississippi in his speech?

____

3 Think about the speeches you have just heard and discuss the following questions in pairs.

1 Do you think gun control laws should be stricter in the United States? Why? What about in other countries?

2 Do you agree with Viola Davis's opinion that everyone should be included when making important decisions? Why?

3 Do you think Martin Luther King, Jr.'s dream came true? Why?

4 Do the speeches refer to issues that are only present in American society? How are these issues relevant for your country and for the rest of the world?

Study Space

5 Select a current issue that is important to you and prepare a speech about it. Remember to:

- think about the audience;
- pick a topic of interest;
- set a goal for your speech;
- do some research on the topic;
- plan your speech (introduction, body and conclusion);
- write your speech.

6 Record a video or an audio of your speech and share it on #MAKERS Digital <www.richmondmakers.com>. Use the hashtag #WhereIStand.

READING

Before Reading

1 **Look at the text and check the best options to answer the questions.**

1 Where can you find texts like this?

a ☐ In government manuals.

b ☐ In newspapers (print or online).

c ☐ In children's magazines.

2 Who might be interested in reading this kind of text?

a ☐ Chinese people and their descendants.

b ☐ Refugees, their families and friends.

c ☐ Anyone who wants to know about the subject.

3 What kind of text is this?

a ☐ It's a piece of news.

b ☐ It's an opinion article.

c ☐ It's a report based on research.

https://www.theguardian.com/commentisfree/2018/feb/02/refugee-crisis-human-flow-ai-weiwei-china

News | Opinion | Sport | Culture | Lifestyle | More

Fri 2 Feb 2018 06.00 GMT

THE REFUGEE CRISIS ISN'T ABOUT REFUGEES. IT'S ABOUT US.

Ai Weiwei

"I was a child refugee", writes the Chinese artist and activist. "I know how it feels to live in a camp, robbed of my humanity. Refugees must be seen to be an essential part of our shared humanity."

Ai Weiwei is a contemporary artist, activist and advocate of political reform in China.

I was born in 1957, the same year China purged more than 300,000 intellectuals, including writers, teachers, journalists and whoever dared to criticize the newly established communist government.

Because my father, Ai Qing, was the most renowned poet in China then, the government made a symbolic example of him. In 1958, my family was forced from our home in Beijing and banished to a "re-education" camp in the most remote area of the country—we had no idea that this was the beginning of a very dark, long journey that would last for two decades.

At the camp, we had to live in an underground dugout and were subjected to unexplainable hatred, discrimination, unprovoked insults and assaults, and as a result, I remember experiencing what felt like endless injustice.

I share this personal background because it sheds light on my emotional connection to the current global refugee condition because I believe these refugees may be feeling as I felt.

Observing, filming a documentary for two years and researching recent and historical refugee events makes some conclusions abundantly clear: not a single refugee we met had willingly left their home. People left their homes because they were forced to by violence, which caused the deaths of family members, relatives and fellow citizens, not to mention entire villages which might vanish under indiscriminate bombing at any moment. There is simply no way for them to stay. Fleeing is the only choice they have to preserve their own lives and the lives of those they love.

A common argument is that many of the people who try to reach the west are economic migrants who wish to take unfair advantage of its prosperity. However, this view ignores the contradiction between today's physical borders and the real political and economic boundaries of our globalised world.

At this moment, the west—which has greatly benefited from globalisation—simply refuses to bear its responsibilities. If we map the 70-plus border walls and fences built between nations in the past three decades, we can see the extent of global economic and political disparities. The people most negatively affected by these walls are the poorest and most desperate of society.

Could physical borders stop refugees? Instead of building walls, we should look at what is causing people to become refugees and work to solve those conditions to stop the flow at its source. To do so will require the most powerful nations in the world to adjust how they are actively shaping the world. How do we think the poor, displaced or occupied can exist when their societies are destroyed? Should they simply disappear? Can we recognise that their continued existence is an essential part of our shared humanity? If we fail to recognise this, how can we speak of "civilised" development?

The refugee crisis is not about refugees, rather, it is about us. Our prioritisation of financial gain over people's struggle for the necessities of life is the primary cause of much of this crisis.

Establishing the understanding that we all belong to one humanity is the most essential step for how we might continue to coexist on this planet. I know what it feels like to be a refugee and to experience the dehumanisation that comes with displacement from home and country. There are many borders to dismantle, but the most important are the ones within our own hearts and minds—these are the borders that are dividing humanity from itself.

Adapted from <https://www.theguardian.com/commentisfree/2018/feb/02/refugee-crisis-human-flow-ai-weiwei-china>. Accessed on July 17, 2018.

While Reading

2 **Read the text and circle the correct answers.**

1 Which are some of the characteristics of this text?
   a It expresses an opinion.
   b It presents facts.
   c It presents information about the author.

2 What is the purpose of this text?
   a To discuss current problems of the world.
   b To express opinions about a subject.
   c To share a personal experience.

3 **Read the article again and check the correct information about its author.**

a [ ] He is an artist, activist and filmmaker.
b [ ] He was a baby when he was sent to a camp.
c [ ] He spent 10 years in the camp with his family.
d [ ] He doesn't feel connected to the current refugee crisis.
e [ ] He has made a documentary.
f [ ] He became a poet in the camp.

4 **Which paragraphs...**

a present a conclusion after observation? ______
b present a background story about the author's life? ______
c present and refute a counterargument? ______
d present an explanation about the title of the text? ______
e present the author's opinion on what should be done? ______

5 **Answer the questions according to the text.**

1 Why was Ai Weiwei's family forced to go to a camp?
______
2 According to the author, what are the reasons people become refugees?
______
3 What is the counterargument the author presents?
______
4 Which alternative does the author present to building walls?
______
5 According to the author, what is the most important step so that we can coexist?
______

6 **The author presents opinions and facts. Identify which sentences express a fact (F) or an opinion (O).**

1 [ ] "[...] not a single refugee we met had willingly left their home."
2 [ ] "People left their homes because they were forced to by violence [...]."
3 [ ] "At this moment, the west [...] simply refuses to bear its responsibilities."
4 [ ] "If we map the 70-plus border walls and fences built between nations in the past three decades, we can see the extent of global economic and political disparities."
5 [ ] "To do so will require the most powerful nations in the world to adjust how they are actively shaping the world."
6 [ ] "If we fail to recognise this, how can we speak of 'civilised' development?"
7 [ ] "Our prioritisation of financial gain over people's struggle for the necessities of life is the primary cause of much of this crisis."
8 [ ] "There are many borders to dismantle, but the most important are the ones within our own hearts and minds [...]."

7 **How did the author find the facts presented in the article?**

______

8 **What does the expression "it sheds light on" in paragraph 4 mean? Underline the correct option.**

a It makes something clear.
b It turns on a light.
c It makes something stand out.

9 **What does the expression "to do so" in paragraph 8 refer to? Underline the correct option.**

a To shape the world differently.
b To make less powerful nations responsible for changes.
c To stop what makes people become refugees.

Study Space

After Reading

10 **Do you agree with Ai Weiwei's opinion on the current refugee crisis? Discuss with a classmate.**

Workbook p. 141

LANGUAGE 2

1 Find and underline in the text on page 42 the sentences that contain *could, might* and *may.*

2 Check what these words express in the sentences you underlined.

a ☐ doubt   b ☒ possibility   c ☐ certainty

Could, Might and *May*

Affirmative

We **could** help refugees with a fundraising campaign.
We **might** coexist more peacefully now that we have talked about the issue.
Colin **may** be willing to take part in the campaign.

Negative

They **could not/couldn't** find a solution to the problem.
The refugee crisis **might not** be unavoidable.
Refugees **may not** feel welcome in some countries.

Interrogative

Could physical borders stop refugees?
Might European countries be willing to help?
May they do something to help those in need?

Short Answers

Yes, they **could/might/may**.
No, they **couldn't/might not/may not**.

Could, ***might*** and ***may*** are used to express possibility.

3 Rewrite the sentences using *could, might* or *may.*

1 The lights are on, so it's possible that they are home.
They may be at home.

2 Paul's accent sounds British, it's not likely that he is from the U.S.
He might don't be from US.

3 It's possible that it will rain tomorrow.
It may rain tomorrow

4 You are possibly right about that.
You could be right.

5 He didn't touch his pasta, so I think he doesn't like it.
He may doesn't like it

6 Her book is open, so she is possibly doing her homework.
She's might doing her homework.

4 Look at the images and write a sentence about each situation using *could, might* or *may.*

1

Anna has been expecting a promotion for a long time, but she didn't get it.
She may/might/could be disappointed.

2

It seems that Rebecca can't find all the money in the cash register.
She might be estressed.

3

Jenna and Mary are taking pictures with hockey fans.
They might be really happy.

4

I gave Fred and Jess a map, but they haven't arrived yet.
They could be lost.

5

Paul usually drives to work, but he came by bus today.
He may be not able to drive his car.

6

Rob, Charles and Harry ordered two large pizzas.
They might be very hungry.

5 Yan and Sean are waiting for their parents' flight to arrive at the airport. Circle the correct options to complete their dialogue.

Yan: Mom and dad's flight was supposed to land at 11 a.m. It's 11:30 now and the flight doesn't appear on the screen. It **may be** / **is certainly** / **isn't** delayed.

Sean: Relax, it's rainy outside, the plane **certainly has** / **might be having** / **isn't having** problems landing.

Yan: You **might be** / **couldn't be** / **aren't** right. At least it isn't snowing, so they **might** / **couldn't be** / **are certainly** stuck in snow.

Sean: I think I'll talk to the airline staff. They **might** / **won't** / **could not** know something.

Yan: Good idea!

A few minutes later...

Sean: The airline staff told me the plane had problems landing because of the weather, but they said it **may** / **might not** / **won't** land soon.

Yan: I hope so... I'm excited to see mom and dad again!

Sean: Me too, but they **will certainly** / **won't** / **couldn't** arrive soon, don't worry.

Yan: Oh, look! Their flight is finally on the screen. It **is going to** / **may not** / **will certainly** be long now.

Sean: Told ya!

6 Answer the questions using *may*, *might* and *could*.

1 What could happen if refugees left the camps?

____

2 What may happen if men and women fight for equality?

It may happen a revolution

3 What may happen if the government doesn't control gun purchase more strictly?

It might be realy dangerous.

Study Space

Too, *Either* and *Neither*

Too, ***either*** and ***neither*** are used to agree with someone.

Agree Affirmatively

Mark: I think refugees should be treated equally.
Claire: I think so **too**.

Agree Negatively

Don: I don't like discussing politics.
Mark: I don't like it **either**.
Claire: **Neither** do I.

7 Write a sentence agreeing with the statements below. Use *too*, *either* or *neither*.

1 **A:** Sarah can't play the violin.
B: Neither do I.

2 **A:** They are wearing jeans.
B: Me too.

3 **A:** I have to study for a test.
B: Me either

4 **A:** I'm not in favor of repatriating refugees.
B: Me too

5 **A:** Emma doesn't speak Chinese.
B: Neither do I

8 19 Listen to some opinions and react to them. You can either agree or disagree with the speaker.

1 ______________________
2 ______________________
3 ______________________
4 ______________________

Pronunciation

9 20 Listen to some words and check the option in each item that is being pronounced.

1 a ☐ read (simple present)
  b ☐ read (simple past)

2 a ☐ close (shut)
  b ☐ close (near)

3 a ☐ lead (guide)
  b ☐ lead (chemical element)

4 a ☐ Polish (nationality)
  b ☐ polish (make shiny)

5 a ☐ bass (fish)
  b ☐ bass (musical instrument)

10 21 Listen to the pairs of words from activity 9. What do the words in each pair have in common? And how are they different?

11 22 Listen again and practice saying the pairs of words in activity 9.

Workbook p. 141

WRITING

An Opinion Article

Before Writing

1 Plan your text.

1 Choose a topic you are interested in and that is relevant to your everyday life to write an opinion article about.

2 Research facts to support your point of view.

3 Plan what to write in each paragraph.

First paragraph: Introduction	Begin your article with a personal anecdote, a rhetorical question or a fact about the topic that will be the focus of your text.
Second paragraph: Argument	Present an opinion on the topic and use facts and examples to support it.
Third paragraph: Counterargument	Present different opinions about the topic and refute them with facts and examples.
Fourth paragraph: Conclusion	Conclude your text by giving your own opinion on the topic.

Drafting

2 Write a draft of your opinion article.

3 Share your text with a classmate and ask for his/her opinion. Make adjustments, if necessary.

Final Writing

4 Write the final version of your opinion article and publish it on #MAKERS Digital <www.richmondmakers.com>. Use the hashtag #TakingAStand.

INVESTIGATE

People in my country are fighting for ____________.

Collect Data

- Think about the most important protests, marches and demonstrations that have taken place in your country recently.
- Research into them and keep a record of the main issues addressed by them. Moreover, find out the number of people that took part in each event. Don't forget to take notes of the following facts:
  - event;
  - type of protest;
  - place;
  - date;
  - number of people;
  - issues addressed.

Analyze the Data

- Were there protests related to human causes? If so, which one(s)?
- Were there protests related to ecological causes? If so, which one(s)?
- Were there protests related to political causes? If so, which one(s)?
- Which protests gathered the biggest number of people?
- Were the protests peaceful?
- How long did the longest protest last?
- Were any of the issues addressed at the events not aligned with the purpose of the protest? If so, which one(s)?

Draw a Conclusion

People in my country are fighting for ____________.

1 Reflect on your conclusion and discuss.

1 What is your opinion about these causes? Are they worth fighting for? Why?

2 Do you support any of these causes? If so, which ones? If not, why?

3 In your opinion, is the way people are protesting effective? Why?

4 Would you take part in a march or demonstration? Why?

2 Share your ideas on #MAKERS Digital <www.richmondmakers.com>. Use the hashtag #ProtestsInMyCountry.

LOCAL AND GLOBAL

1 Read the headlines and answer the questions below.

1 Google's top news link for "final election results" goes to a fake news site with false numbers

Available at <https://www.washingtonpost.com/news/the-fix/wp/2016/11/14/googles-top-news-link-for-final-election-results-goes-to-a-fake-news-site-with-false-numbers/?utm_term=.84deb3319abf>. Accessed on July 20, 2018.

2 Antisocial woman pretends to be blind for 28 years so she wouldn't have to greet people

Available at <http://www.odditycentral.com/news/antisocial-woman-pretends-to-be-blind-for-28-years-so-she-wouldnt-have-to-greet-people.html>. Accessed on July 20, 2018.

3 How China used more cement in 3 years than the U.S. did in the entire 20th century

Available at <https://www.washingtonpost.com/news/wonk/wp/2015/03/24/how-china-used-more-cement-in-3-years-than-the-u-s-did-in-the-entire-20th-century/?noredirect=on&utm_term=.00bf8c29e734>. Accessed on July 20, 2018.

4 Canada: passenger allowed onto flight after security confiscate his bomb

Available at <https://www.bbc.com/news/blogs-news-from-elsewhere-25760132>. Accessed on July 20, 2018.

5 Harambe, a dead gorilla, got over 15,000 votes for president of the United States

Available at <https://www.snopes.com/fact-check/harambe-15000-votes/>. Accessed on July 20, 2018.

a Two of these headlines are fake and three of them are true. Which ones sound fake to you?

b Research the headlines on the internet. Which ones are true? How do you know that?

c How can you check if a piece of news is fake or not?

2 Research and answer the questions to find out if this headline is fake or not.

Trump offering free one-way tickets to Africa & Mexico for those who wanna leave America

Available at <http://www.qatarday.com/blog/information/trump-offering-free-one-way-tickets-to-africa-/22094>. Accessed on July 20, 2018.

1 Do you think this headline sounds reasonable? Why?

2 Did you find it on more than one website?

3 Were the sources where you found it trustworthy?

4 Does the news item present reliable sources to where the headline was taken from?

3 Discuss the questions in small groups.

1 Is fake news harmless?

2 What are the dangers of sharing fake news?

3 How could you educate people on how to check if a news item is real before sharing it?

IMAGINE

Imagine not having to discuss controversial issues.

1 Research into the concept. Bring your research to be discussed in class.

2 Read the text and discuss with a classmate.

RTV

1 How important do you think it is to have an opinion and take a stand?

2 Do you agree with Dan Brown's quote? Why?

3 Did any piece of information surprise you? If so, what?

4 Do you think these facts are useful whenever discussing a subject? Why?

4

STAY HEALTHY

OBJECTIVES

- Discuss different things people can do to stay healthy.
- Talk about how important a balanced diet is for a healthy life.
- Connect laughter to its impact on our lives.
- Read two infographics and reflect on the importance of mental well-being.
- Create an infographic encouraging people to stay healthy.
- Reflect on the impact of bullying on people's lives.

Read the questions and discuss.

1. How important do you think relaxing and having time for yourself is?
2. What do you do when you want to relax?
3. Is keeping a healthy diet part of your habits?
4. Do you practice any physical activities? Why?

Richmond

#MAKERS DIGITAL

1

2

3

4

5

RTV

1 **Match the images on page 50 to the free-time activities.**

a ☐ do yoga
b ☐ hang out with your friends
c ☐ spend time with your family
d ☐ write a journal
e ☐ play with a pet

2 **Now answer the questions.**

1 Do you do any of these things to relax? Which one(s)?
2 Which of them do you find most effective to help you relax? Why?
3 What other things do you like to do in your free time to unwind?

3 **Lucrecia has a hobby that helps her express her feelings. Watch the video and check what she does.**

1 ☐ writes novels
2 ☐ writes poems
3 ☐ writes plays
4 ☐ writes in her journal

4 **Watch the video again and answer the questions.**

1 What does Lucrecia do when she feels angry or sad?

2 What was Lucrecia like when she was young?

3 Does Lucrecia find it easy to talk about her feelings?

4 How does Lucrecia help people who have experienced similar situations?

5 Lucrecia helps run a charity. What does it do?

5 **Would you like to join Lucrecia in her charity work? Why?**

Makerspace p. 115

React!

6 **Read the comments. Then write your own opinion on the video.**

Paul Kepler I guess a program that uses poetry to help people would be successful here in Richmond. #poetryhelps
39 min

Poesy & Poetry Poetry is life! I wanna read some of her poems. I loved the one she recited in the video.
27 min

Bookworm I don't mind reading poetry, but I can't write it. Words disappear whenever I try to write something.
13 min

Music Leah I really don't like poetry. #wasteoftime I prefer to express my feelings through music. I play the piano and it really helps me.
5 min

POST

I Wonder

7 **Write a question about healthy ways of dealing with feelings. Then look for the answer.**

99 Great! 99 Interact

LANGUAGE 1

1 Analyze the charts and complete them with the words that are missing.

Verb	Noun
	laugh; laughter
relax	
express	
	meditation

Adjective	Noun
anxious	
	health
active	
	stress

2 Complete the leaflet using some of the words from the charts in activity 1.

Keeping your body (and mind) fit!

We spend a lot of time looking at screens: our smartphones, our computer, our TV. How about some offline time to keep our mind and body fit? Here are some ideas:

1. Get enough sleep

Sleeping at least 8 hours a day helps our body (1) ____________ and get ready for another day! Some people practice (2) ____________ for a few minutes before going to bed to help them in the (3) ____________ process.

2. Understand and express your feelings

Don't be afraid to (4) ____________ your emotions. But for you to do that, you first need to understand your feelings. (5) ____________ often, show gratitude, talk to loved ones and ask for help to deal with difficult situations. These (6) ____________ will help you manage (7) ____________, feel more confident and face your fears.

3. Stay active!

Staying active is very important for your body and your mind. Practicing physical activities is essential, but don't forget that eating well, spending time outside and getting a bit of sunshine are all part of staying (8) ____________. People who are active have better self-esteem and are better able to control (9) ____________. You can also find a quiet place and (10) ____________ after your physical activities to help you recover your energy and clear your mind.

Based on <https://oedb.org/ilibrarian/100-ways-to-keep-your-mind-healthy/>; <https://www.leanbodyforher.com/articles/10-ways-to-keep-your-mind-fit/>. Accessed on July 30, 2018.

3 Look at the relaxation activities below. Then follow the example and use some words from activity 2 to explain the advantages of each one.

1

laughing

Laughing is an effective way to control your anxiety. It's also a good way to relax and manage stress.

2

meditation

3

cooking

4

playing with pets

5

writing poetry

6

listening to music

Study Space   My Glossary

4 Which of the relaxation activities from activity 3 do you do when you want to relax? Which activities do you think are not ideal for you?

5 Answer the questions with your own ideas.

1 How important is it to stay active?
2 Is showing gratitude part of your habits?
3 How do you manage stress?
4 What do you do to keep a good level of self-esteem?
5 How do you deal with difficult situations?

LISTENING AND SPEAKING

1 23 **Listen to a debate on a radio show and check the correct options.**

1 The radio program is about ______.

a ☐ how laughing can improve our health

b ☐ the disadvantages of laughing too much

2 The doctors ______ that laughter is the best medicine.

a ☐ agree b ☐ disagree

3 Laughing can have a ______ impact on people's mood.

a ☐ positive b ☐ negative

2 24 **Listen to the debate again and correct the sentences according to it.**

1 Tamara Richards and Jonathan York are both university professors.

____

2 According to some research, laughing has no effect if it's not genuine.

____

3 Laughing will only benefit your mental health.

____

4 Studies from the University of Oxford show that laughing too hard is the best medicine.

____

5 Laughter can help people express their feelings and think faster.

____

3 **Who used each of these arguments? Write *Dr. Richards* or *Dr. York*.**

1 Laughter has mental, physical and social benefits. ______

2 Fake laughter doesn't have the same benefits as genuine laughter. ______

3 It's important to investigate the benefits of laughter a little more. ______

4 Laughing burns calories. ______

5 Sometimes a bit of me time might be just as helpful. ______

4 **Do you agree with Dr. Richards or with Dr. York? Why?**

Buzzwords

"Sometimes a bit of ***me time*** *is just as helpful."*

What does "me time" mean? Look it up!

Pronunciation

5 25 **Listen to the audio and complete the sentence with the words you hear.**

It (1) ______ to fight (2) ______ heart disease, (3) ______.

6 **Think and answer these questions.**

1 Does Dr. York pronounce all the words in the sentence?

2 Which letters are linked?

7 **Identify and circle possible consonant sound + vowel sound connections in the pronunciation of these sentences.**

1 Being physically active protects against mental health problems.

2 Being physically active decreases depression in older adults.

3 Being physically active is as effective as medication to relieve anxiety.

4 People who participate in sports clubs and organized recreational activities enjoy better mental health.

8 26 **Now listen to the sentences in activity 7 and check your answers. Then practice saying them.**

9 **You are going to have a debate about the following statement: "You should not practice sports if you don't have the assistance of a professional".**

- Write two lists of arguments: one for and another against this idea.
- Research what different people say about it.
- Organize your debate and decide who will be for and who will be against the practice of sports without professional supervision.
- Make sure you choose a mediator.

10 **Record your debate and share it on #MAKERS Digital <www.richmondmakers.com>. Use the hashtag #StayFit.**

Study Space

READING

Before Reading

1 What kind of texts are these?

2 Scan the titles of both texts and answer: what are they about?

1

Physical activity and mental health

Being physically active:

Protects against mental health problems

Decreases depression in older adults

Reduces the symptoms of post-natal depression

Is as effective as medication for mild to moderate anxiety and depression

Improves self-esteem and cognitive function in young people

People who participate in sports clubs and organized recreational activities enjoy better mental health

Playing sport reduces psychological distress by **34%** (1–3 times a week) **47%** (4+ times a week)

Our whole community wins

Adapted from the infographic "Physical activity and mental health", by the Government of Western Australia.

2

Things you need to know about mental well-being

- Eating well
- Caring for others
- Learning new skills
- Keeping physically active
- Talking about your feelings
- Valuing yourself and others
- Keeping in touch with friends and loved ones
- Taking a break
- Doing something creative
- Asking for help

Mental health promotion involves any action to enhance the mental well-being of individuals[4]

Evidence shows that mental health promotion can contribute to the prevention of common mental health problems[4]

76% of NHS trusts report that they monitor the well-being of their staff.[1]

3 in 4 people suffering from mental illness get no treatment at all.[2]

50% of adult mental illnesses starts before the age of 15.[2]

8-12% of the population experience depression in any year.[4]

Mental ill health at work is thought to cost UK employers **£26 billion** each year.[3]

NHS organisations should:

- Have a strategic and coordinated approach to promoting employees' mental well-being and assessing risk.
- Strengthen the role of line managers in promoting employee mental well-being.

SOURCES

1. http://www.rcplondon.ac.uk/resources/nice-public-health-guidance-workplace-organisational-audit
2. http://www.acas.org.uk/media/pdf/n/t/Is-it-time-wellbeing-grew-up.pdf
3. www.centreformentalhealth.org.uk/pdfs/mental_health_at_work.pdf
4. http://www.mentalhealth.org.uk/content/assets/PDF/publications/fundamental_facts_2007.pdf?view=Standard

Adapted from <http://www.nhsemployers.org/~/media/Employers/Documents/Retain%20and%20improve/MentalHealth%20Infographic%20WEB%20FINAL.pdf>. Accessed on July 31, 2018.

While Reading

3 **Read the infographics and check the verbal and nonverbal elements you find in them.**

1 ☐ photos
2 ☐ facts
3 ☐ figures
4 ☐ long texts
5 ☐ images
6 ☐ personal opinion
7 ☐ charts
8 ☐ sources

4 **Scan the infographics and check the statements that are right for both of them. Then correct the ones that are wrong.**

1 ☐ They have detailed academic texts with references. ______________

2 ☐ The images are used to convey a message.
____

3 ☐ They don't have any data. ______________

4 ☐ The images and the texts are connected.
____

5 **Read the first infographic. Then correct the sentences according to what you read.**

1 Being mentally active protects against physical problems.
____

2 Being physically active decreases depression in younger adults and improves self-esteem and cognitive function in older people.
____

3 If you play sports, you reduce psychological distress by 47%.
____

6 **Read the second infographic and complete the sentences.**

1 Mental health initiatives can contribute to the __________ of mental health problems.

2 Eating well and taking a break are among the __________ that can enhance mental well-being.

3 __________ in four people suffering from mental illness gets treatment.

4 24% of NHS trusts don't really monitor the __________ of their staff.

5 Half of adult mental __________ starts before people turn 15.

7 **Which ideas from the infographics on page 54 do these images represent? Write them down.**

1

2

3

4

After Reading

8 **How important are these things for you? Rank them from 1 (least important) to 7 (most important).**

a ☐ participating in a sports club
b ☐ getting enough sleep
c ☐ doing something creative
d ☐ taking a break from studying
e ☐ being outdoors
f ☐ asking for help
g ☐ keeping in touch with friends and loved ones

9 **Use the ideas from the infographics to complete the questions below. Then answer them so that they are true for you.**

1 How often do you ______________?
____

2 When was the last time you ______________?
____

3 Why do you think ______________ is important?
____

Study Space
Workbook p. 143

LANGUAGE 2

1 **Circle all the verbs you find in the sentences below.**

1 If you learn new skills, you feel better about yourself.

2 When you talk about your feelings, you face your fears.

3 Your self-esteem doesn't really improve unless you take care of your physical and mental health.

4 Physical exercise is highly recommended provided that you don't overdo it.

2 **Look at the sentences in activity 1 and answer the questions.**

1 What do the sentences have in common?

____

2 What is the tense of the verbs you circled?

____

3 Do the sentences express a possible future or a natural consequence?

____

4 If you change the order of the clauses, does the information change?

____

Zero Conditional

In the zero conditional, both parts of the sentence are in the simple present tense. Also, the word *if* can usually be replaced by the word *when* without any change in meaning.
The zero conditional is used in the following circumstances:

- when the situation is real and possible;

  If you **do** creative activities that you enjoy, you **enhance** your mental well-being.

- to describe general truths.

  When you **heat** water, it **boils**.

The *if* clause is formed by *if/when* + present tense. When the sentence starts with *if/when*, we use a comma:

If you **have** time to relax, you **improve** your life quality.

You **improve** your life quality if you **have** time to relax.

Snack Learning

Besides the linking words *if* and *when*, we can also use:

- **provided that:** means the same as *if*, but it is usually used in more formal contexts.

  You can run a marathon **provided that** you respect your limits.

- **unless:** means the same as *if not*.

  If the plants **don't** get enough water, they don't survive.
  Unless the plants get enough water, they don't survive

3 **Complete the statements with the correct form of the verbs in parentheses to express general truths.**

1 It's a fact of life: if you do physical exercise frequently, your body _______ (get) stronger.

2 When you are too stressed out, you _______ (have) headaches constantly. It's a natural consequence.

3 People get stressed out unless they _______ (stop) thinking about their obligations for a while.

4 When you do yoga, you _______ (relieve) stress. It always works this way.

5 If you _______ (have) a well-balanced diet, your body feels better.

4 **Use the prompts to create zero conditionals.**

1 if / public transport / be efficient → people / stop using their cars

If public transport is efficient, people stop using their cars.

2 when / freeze water → become solid

____

3 get purple → when / mix red and blue

____

4 unless / my mother / be home → I / take calls

____

5 if / it / rain → physical education classes / happen / in the gym

____

5 **In your notebook, rewrite the sentences from activity 4 using a different linking word.**

1 Provided that public transport is efficient, people stop using their cars.

6 Read Hernandez and Lisa talking about the infographics. Then underline all the sentences that express both a condition and its result.

Hernandez: I had absolutely no idea that mental illness problems can start before the age of 15!

Lisa: I know! This was quite a surprise for me too. But if the government keeps promoting information and programs about mental well-being, the number of people suffering from mental illness might drop.

Hernandez: I agree that the government plays a major role in preventing mental illnesses. But we can also share some of this information with our friends. For example, now I know that if you start doing creative activities, you will probably feel better about life in general. Extra points for our creativity courses!

Lisa: Absolutely! And you may also enhance your well-being provided that you eat well and keep physically fit. These are things we can do at school.

Hernandez: Physical activities seem to be closely related to our mental well-being, right? I guess I'll start practicing more sports after class unless you invite me to practice sports with you on the weekends...

7 Look at the underlined sentences in activity 6. Then circle the best option to complete the statements below.

1. They all have **verbs** / **linking words** to express a condition.
2. Modal verbs **can** / **can't** be used to express a probable result.
3. The auxiliary verb **will** / **do** can be used to talk about probable results.
4. They describe a **general truth** / **future possibility**.

First Conditional

The first conditional is used to talk about real and possible situations in the present or in the future.
You **might feel** better **if** you **keep** exercising.
Unless we **take** a break once in a while, we **won't be able to** think straight.
If the government **keeps** promoting programs about mental health, the situation **will improve**.

8 Match the two parts of the conditionals.

1. If we heat ice, ...
2. I'll finish my assignment today...
3. When it rains, ...
4. People might feel better...
5. Unless you hurry, ...
6. If I have time, ...

a ☐ unless I need to help my parents with the house chores.

b ☐ if they talk to their friends and family more often.

c ☐ it melts.

d ☐ I'll buy the groceries.

e ☐ you'll miss the school bus.

f ☐ the street in front of my house floods.

9 Look at the images and write a conditional sentence about each of them.

1

2

1. ______________________
2. ______________________

10 Answer the questions.

1. What do you do when you have free time?
____
2. If you find some money on the floor, what will you do?
____
3. Who do you talk to when you are not feeling well?
____
4. If foreign students arrive at your school, what will you do to welcome them?
____
5. Where do you usually go if you want to have some me time?
____

Study Space   Workbook p. 143

WRITING

An Infographic About Wellness

Before Writing

1 Consider the items below to plan your infographic.

1. Look up different infographics about well-being in different sources: magazines, websites, newspapers.
2. How are you going to select the sources of information?
3. Why did this infographic catch your attention? What features can you identify in it?
4. What is the target audience of your infographic?
5. What information is relevant for your infographic?
6. What is the layout of your infographic going to be like?
7. Are you going to use images, drawings and/or charts?
8. What is the purpose of the nonverbal elements that you will use?
9. What message do you want these verbal and nonverbal elements to convey?
10. How are you going to share your infographic?

Drafting

2 In your notebook, make a draft of your infographic. If you don't have the images yet, write a brief description of them.

3 Share your draft with a classmate and ask for his/her opinion. Make adjustments, if necessary.

Final Writing

4 Make the final version of your infographic and share it on #MAKERS Digital <www.richmondmakers.com>. Use the hashtag #Wellness.

INVESTIGATE

Few Some Most

__________ of the people I know consider themselves mentally healthy.

Collect Data

- Investigate what being mentally healthy is.
- Refer to your research to complete the definition "You are mentally healthy when/if..." in your notebook.
- Interview at least six friends or family members.
- Take notes on their answers and ask follow-up questions to investigate reasons.
- Add up the number of people who consider themselves mentally healthy.

Analyze the Data

- How many people consider themselves mentally healthy?
- What reasons did people give for their answers?
- How did their answers compare to your own perception of their feelings?
- Did the reasons people give you match your perception of their answers?
- How do your results compare with the results of your classmates?

Draw a Conclusion

Few Some Most

__________ of the people I know consider themselves mentally healthy.

1 Reflect on your conclusions and discuss.

1. Are there reasons for people to feel mentally unhealthy in your community?
2. Was there anything unexpected in the results?
3. What suggestions could you give to your interviewees for them to improve their mental health?

2 Share your ideas on #MAKERS Digital <www.richmondmakers.com>. Use the hashtag #MentalHealth.

LOCAL AND GLOBAL

WHAT IS BULLYING?

Bullying is when someone is hurt either by words or actions on purpose, usually more than once, feels bad because of it and has a hard time stopping what is happening to them.

Bullying can be physical or emotional. If you hit, push, yell at or take things from other people, you are bullying them. You are also a bully when you make fun of someone or laugh at people.

Bullying is linked to many negative outcomes including impact on mental health and can affect everyone involved—the bullied and the bullies. Kids who are bullied can experience negative physical, school and mental health issues. Those who bully others can also engage in violent and other risky behaviors into adulthood.

Unfortunately, bullying can happen anywhere. It can occur in your neighborhood, while going to school, at school and even online (cyberbullying).

If we don't talk about bullying, it will never stop. If we can't stop it, many people will keep suffering unnecessarily.

Based on <https://www.stopbullying.gov/at-risk/effects/index.html>; <https://www.pacerkidsagainstbullying.org/what-is-bullying/>. Accessed on July 30, 2018.

1 Read the text and discuss the questions with a classmate.

1. Is bullying a problem in your country?
2. Why do you think this problem often happens at school?
3. Do you know anyone who has been a victim of bullying?

2 Research facts and figures about bullying in your country and in the world. Consider the following:

- statistics about cases of bullying;
- most frequent types of bullying;
- consequences for people who suffer bullying;
- successful campaigns against bullying.

3 Share your findings with your schoolmates and consider communication strategies to raise awareness of the dangers of bullying.

IMAGINE

Imagine life without emotions.

1 Research into the concept. Bring your findings to be discussed in class.

2 Read the magazine article. Then discuss the questions with a classmate.

RTV

1. How important is it for you to be able to express your feelings?
2. Is expressing feelings part of your culture?
3. How would you feel if you couldn't express your feelings?

REVIEW 3

1 Complete the conversation between Anna and Paul about compulsory voting with the expressions from the box.

fair enough from my point of view
I agree with you
I have a completely different opinion on that
I have a feeling that I see what you're saying
that's a fair point

Anna: Paul, you think that voting shouldn't be compulsory. Why is that?

Paul: Well, (1) ______________________, forcing people to vote is not very democratic.

Anna: (2) ______________________, but if voting weren't compulsory, very few people would vote, don't you think?

Paul: (3) ______________________, but the few people who would vote would do it right, because they would do it willingly.

Anna: (4) ______________________. I think there is no right or wrong way to vote.

Paul: OK, I may have expressed myself wrongly, but (5) ______________________ many people who vote because they have to don't even know their candidate's political position.

Anna: (6) ______________________! I just think that, since politicians rule for everyone, everyone should vote to choose them.

Paul: (7) ______________________.

2 Match the sentences.

1 This couldn't be James' bag.
2 Sue may be at piano practice now.
3 You may not be able to talk to my teacher.
4 This may be the new student.
5 This might not be our class.
6 I could call you later.

a [ ] I've heard he's on sick leave.
b [ ] I've never seen him here before.
c [ ] This one is blue and his is green.
d [ ] What time will you be free?
e [ ] Her lessons are always in the morning.
f [ ] The students are too young!

3 Sue and Zack are watching TV. Circle the correct options to complete their conversation.

Sue: Do you know what this commercial is about? Oh, wait, it (1) **might be** / **is** about a movie. I've seen this actor before.

Zack: No, it (2) **couldn't** / **may** be about a movie because they are singing a rap song!

Sue: You're right! It (3) **is** / **may be** about a rap album or something. I'm still not sure...

Zack: I think it (4) **can't** / **might** be about something completely different. Those Super Bowl commercials are always like this.

Sue: Yes, you (5) **could be** / **are** right, I guess.

Zack: Look, Sue! I can't believe it! It (6) **is** / **could be** a chips commercial!

Sue: True! It does catch our attention, doesn't it?

4 Complete the sentences with *too*, *neither* or *either*.

1 **A:** I haven't finished my homework yet.
B: I haven't ________.

2 **A:** I can speak English.
B: I can speak English ________.

3 **A:** I didn't travel during my last vacation.
B: ________ did I.

4 **A:** I haven't seen this movie yet.
B: I haven't seen it ________.

5 React to the sentences below. You can agree or disagree with them.

1 Sarah loves ice cream.
____

2 We haven't seen the latest Star Wars movies.
____

3 I think teenagers should have more freedom.
____

4 We are living in an apartment now.
____

REVIEW 4

1 27 **Listen to two friends deciding on a holiday trip and check the correct options.**

1 If they go to the mountains, ...
- a ☐ Chris will be really happy about it.
- b ☐ Chris might be disappointed.
- c ☐ Chris will help with the organization of a surfing trip.

2 Unless they go somewhere chilly, ...
- a ☐ Chris won't join them.
- b ☐ Kyle will be happy and pleased.
- c ☐ Kyle will not travel with them.

3 They might not find a hotel...
- a ☐ if they decide to go to a beach.
- b ☐ if they choose to travel to the mountains.
- c ☐ unless they decide the destination fast.

4 Kyle gets upset...
- a ☐ when things are different from what he wants.
- b ☐ if Chris goes surfing.
- c ☐ when Greg and Marcello choose the travel destination.

5 If they find a city with a lake, ...
- a ☐ Chris will choose to go surfing on his own.
- b ☐ Chris might join them.
- c ☐ Chris will learn how to do stand-up paddling.

6 They always have a good time...
- a ☐ when they are with their friends.
- b ☐ if Chris and Kyle manage to compromise.
- c ☐ when they go to the mountains.

2 **Use the nouns below (or their corresponding verb or adjective) to write sentences related to Marcello and Greg's conversation.**

1 (relaxation) Greg is anxious to chill and relax.

2 (stress) ______

3 (laughter) ______

4 (action) ______

3 **Complete the sentences with the correct form of the verbs in parentheses.**

1 Her mother will be upset if she ______ (go) to the movies by herself.

2 If he ______ (keep) working so hard with no time to relax, he might ruin his health.

3 I ______ (allow) you to take my headphones if you promise to take good care of them.

4 Danny will visit us if he ______ (be) too busy.

5 Unless we ______ (work) together, we will never finish this project on time.

6 If you ______ (send) this package by mail today, she will get it in two days.

7 When you study on a regular basis, your results ______ (improve).

8 Deborah ______ (spend) her summer holidays with her grandma if she saves enough money.

9 Unless you stop drinking coffee now, you ______ (be) able to sleep.

10 If you need any help, just ______ (give) me a call.

4 **Look at the images and complete the sentences about the benefits of these activities for mental health.**

1

Unless you meditate more often, ______.

2

When you adopt a pet ______.

3

You might be more productive ______.

4

If you express your gratitude, ______.

5

MORE THAN MEETS THE EYE

OBJECTIVES

- Comment and give opinions on different kinds of visual arts.
- Understand the content of an audio guide.
- Present a piece of art.
- Understand the main characteristics of an online discussion forum.
- Write a post for an online discussion forum.
- Talk about hypothetical situations.
- Reflect on who should own an artwork.
- Reflect on the idea of looking like a painting.

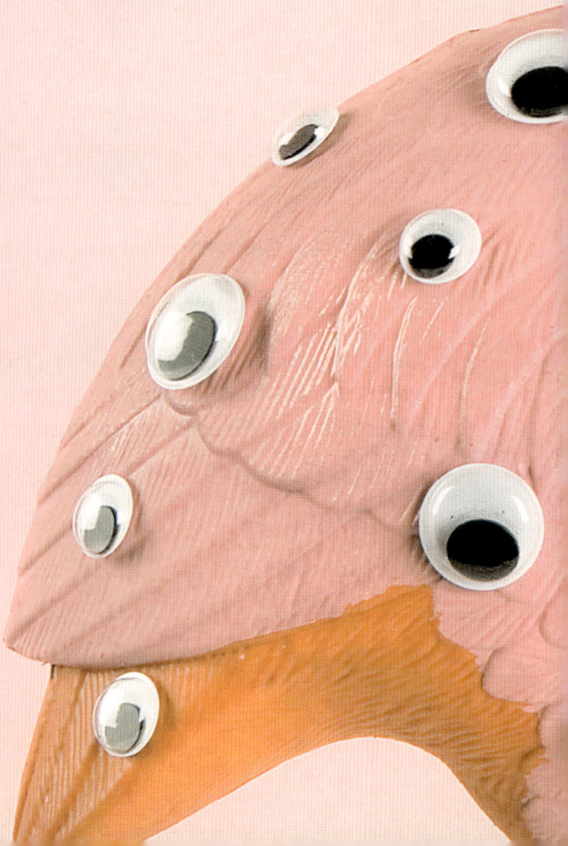

Read the questions and discuss.

1 What comes to your mind when you think of art?
2 In your opinion, what can be considered art?
3 Which kinds of visual art do you know?
4 What comes to mind when you look at this image?

Richmond

#MAKERS
DIGITAL

1

2

3

4

5

RTV

1 Look at the tools and materials on page 64. Then match them to the kinds of art in which they are used.

architecture   design   graffiti   movie
painting   photography   sculpture

1 Image 1: graffiti
2 Image 2: painting
3 Image 3: photography
4 Image 4: sculpture
5 Image 5: design

2 Which of the tools and materials in the images would you use to express your creativity? Why?

3 Watch the video about a competition in which artists put their creativity to the test. What kind of artists are they?

4 Watch the video again and answer the questions.

1 What do the artists have to do? ______
2 What can't the judges know? ______
3 How much time do they have to do their work? ______
4 For the judges, how is creativity shown? ______
5 Who won the competition? ______

5 What do you think about the artwork chosen by the judges? Do you agree it was the best?

6 Look at the images on page 64 again. Which one portrays the material used by the artists during this competition?

React!

7 Write a comment about the video.

ArtsyMark This competition is awesome! I wish we had something like that in my country. I want to take part in it!

BillyC2002 This is such a gr8 way of expressing our creativity! I'm taking pottery classes once a week, but I still can't do all the things these guys do.

BTWMonique It's gr8 to see a pottery competition! This is much harder than U could imagine! I've tried it once and it was a total disaster! So I decided to stick to taking my pictures. LOL!

______
______

I Wonder

8 Write a question about visual arts. Then look for the answer.

______
______

99 Great!   99 Interact

LANGUAGE 1

1 **Match the sentence halves.**

1 Although my dad doesn't like it, I'm really fond
2 I don't know much about design, but I'm interested
3 Rodin is famous
4 Joseph is good
5 I wouldn't be a good architect because I'm really bad
6 I'm excited
7 Neil Patrick Harris is known
8 She doesn't want to be remembered

a [ ] for being an actor, but he's also a magician.
b [ ] of graffiti.
c [ ] at drawing.
d [ ] for her beauty only. She's also a talented photographer.
e [ ] for the sculpture *The Thinker*.
f [ ] in it.
g [ ] about starting my photography course.
h [ ] at painting portraits.

2 **Look at the sentences formed in activity 1 and complete the collocations with the correct prepositions.**

1 fond ______
2 interested ______
3 famous ______
4 good ______
5 bad ______
6 excited ______
7 known ______
8 remembered ______

3 **Complete the opinions about different movie genres using the adjectives and prepositions from activity 2.**

1 Thrillers give the viewer a feeling of suspense. Hitchcock, for example, was very ______ making them. I think he's the best.
2 I think horror movies are too frightening. They are ______ being popular among younger people, so maybe I'm too old for them.
3 I'm ______ comedies. I have a very stressful routine, so I like to watch movies that help me unwind.
4 I'm usually not ______ musicals, but I had fun watching *La La Land*. I guess Emma Stone will always be ______ her role in this movie.

Study Space

4 **Complete the blog post with the correct prepositions.**

about at (2x) for (3x) in ~~of~~

www.richmond.com.br

If you're fond (1) ______ photography, you probably know Sebastião Salgado. He is known (2) ______ his black-and-white photographs of people in difficult situations around the world. He's really good (3) ______ what he does. Maybe that's why there are so many people interested (4) ______ his work. Curiously, although Salgado is famous (5) ______ his photographs, he began his career as an economist. Why did he decide to change careers? Maybe he was excited (6) ______ expressing himself artistically through photography and having an impact on the world. The fact is that he'll always be remembered (7) ______ his art.

Based on <https://www.biography.com/people/sebastião-salgado-40046>. Accessed on August 2, 2018.

My Glossary

5 **Complete the sentences so that they are true for you. Use an adjective and a preposition from the previous activities and your own ideas.**

1 I'm proud of the poems I write.
2 My parents are ______.
3 My best friend is ______.
4 My classmates are ______.
5 My English teacher is ______.

6 **Complete the sentences so that they are true for you.**

1 I'm good at ______.
2 I'm interested in ______.
3 I'm fond of ______.
4 I want to be remembered for ______.
5 I'm excited about ______.

LISTENING AND SPEAKING

1 Look at the image and answer the questions.

1 What kind of museum is this? ______________

2 Do you like this kind of museum? ______________

3 How often do you go to museums? ______________

4 Do you ever listen to audio guides when you are at a museum? Why? ______________

5 What kind of information do you expect to hear in an audio guide? ______________

2 28 Listen to the audio guide. Which of these artworks is it about?

a ☐

b ☐

c ☐

d ☐

3 29 Listen to the audio guide again and check all the pieces of information that are mentioned.

a ☐ name of the artwork

b ☐ name of the artist

c ☐ when it was exhibited for the first time

d ☐ critics' opinion at the time it was made

e ☐ value of the artwork

f ☐ when the museum bought it

4 30 Listen to the audio guide one more time and complete the fact file.

Name of the artwork: The Little Fourteen-Year-Old Dancer
Artist: Edgar ______________
First exhibition (year): ______________
First exhibition (place): ______________
Was the critics' initial reception positive or negative? ______________
Is it popular nowadays? ______________
Model's name: Marie van Goethem
Model's occupation: ______________
Original material: ______________, horse hair and cloth
Originally compared to: ______________ in shop windows and wax work figures from ethnographic museums

5 What's your opinion about *The Little Fourteen-Year-Old Dancer*?

Study Space

6 Research a work of art. Use the questions below to help you and take notes of your findings.

1 Does this artwork have a name? If so, what is it?
____

2 When was it made?
____

3 What is it made of?
____

4 What do you know about the context in which it was made?
____

5 What do you know about its history?
____

6 What do you think people would like to know about it?
____

7 Present the work of art you chose as if you were a tour guide. You can use the expressions in the box to help you.

This is... It's made of...
It shows/represents... It's interesting because...
It was made by... in...

8 Record your audio guide about the artwork you chose and share it on #MAKERS Digital <www.richmondmakers.com>. Use the hashtag #AudioGuide.

READING

Before Reading

1 Look at the text. What type of text is it?

#makersforum

HOME | TALK | CONTACT SEARCH

Art assignment due next week, HELP!!!

PatsyGraph

I'm taking an art course and the final assignment is to make a portrait. I've decided to create a digital portrait of my grandma in cubist style. Which tools should I use to produce the cubist effect I want?

JoeCool2000

@PatsyGraph It's a great idea to make a cubist artwork! But a digital portrait? Shouldn't you use paper and pencils or brushes? I mean, this digital stuff is not reeeally art, is it? Cuz it's all just ctrl + c/ctrl + v. If I had to make a portrait, I would stick to real art.

AnnPaint

@JoeCool2000 Not true! It takes a lot of effort and skill to create something like that! There are lots of digital art exhibitions and even digital art galleries. You should check them out! @PatsyGraph I'm sure that's going to be a gr8 project! I would use a graphic tablet and a stylus pen if I had access to them. Can you share your final work with us? I'd love to see the pics!

PatsyGraph

@AnnPaint Tks for the suggestion! I guess I can borrow a tablet and a stylus pen from school. I'll share some pics of my work here!

Design_Tom

@JoeCool2000 Have you heard of the Digital Art Museum (http://www.dam.org/)? All the pieces they display have been digitally created. You'll see some blinding works of art there! I personally luv 3-D printers, you can sketch pretty much anything and then print it, even sculptures! @PatsyGraph You can also use image-editing software and graphic design software to complement your work.

JoeCool2000

@AnnPaint and @Design_Tom Wow! I've checked out the DAM website and their pieces are super cool! Sorry if I offended anyone, it wasn't my intention. @PatsyGraph Ur project's gonna be awesome! Good luck!

2 Discuss the questions with a classmate.

1 What do you think people usually talk about on online forums?

2 Do you ever take part in online discussion forums? Why?

3 What would motivate you to reply to a post on an online forum?

4 What would motivate you to post or start a topic on an online forum?

3 Which of the following are characteristics of an online discussion forum?

a ☐ Participants have to use their real names.

b ☒ Participants may not use real pictures of themselves.

c ☐ Participants have to be formal because this is a written text.

d ☒ Participants usually use informal language and abbreviations.

e ☒ Participants usually post questions for other participants to answer.

f ☒ Participants can include hyperlinks to other webpages.

g ☒ Participants can disagree with each other, but they should be respectful.

h ☒ Participants use "@" to direct their messages at specific participants.

While Reading

4 Read the title of the discussion thread. What type of help does the user need?

Buying art.

5 Read the posts again and complete the sentences with the correct username: *PatsyGraph*, *JoeCool2000*, *AnnPaint* or *Design_Tom*.

1 AnnPaint thinks that people need talent and hard work to produce digital art.

2 AnnPaint and Design_Tom disagree with JoeCool2000.

3 JoeCool changes his opinion about digital art.

4 PatsyGraph is going to post pictures of her work.

5 Design_Tom recommends a digital art museum.

6 AnnPaint recommends some equipment.

7 Design_Tom recommends some software.

6 Answer the questions according to the discussion in the forum.

1 What style of art does PatsyGraph want to use in her portrait?

Digital art.

2 What is JoeCool2000's initial opinion about digital art?

He thinks that's not real art

3 What is the DAM?

It's a website.

4 What can you do with a 3-D painter?

You can sketch and print it.

7 Use words from the discussion thread to label the objects.

Buzzwords

*"You'll see some **blinding** works of art there!"*

What does "blinding" mean? Look it up!

8 Make a list of things you consider blinding and share it with a classmate.

1 __________

2 __________

3 __________

Study Space

After Reading

9 What suggestion would you give to PatsyGraph?

10 Take a look at the works of art on the DAM (Digital Art Museum) and discuss the questions with a classmate.

1 What do you think about digital art? Is it real art?

2 Do you like the works on the DAM?

3 Choose one of the works on the DAM. What comes to your mind when you look at it?

Workbook p. 145

LANGUAGE 2

Snack Learning

Internet Abbreviations

cuz = because	pics = pictures
gr8 = great	tks = thanks
luv = love	ur = your

1 **Make the comment below more informal by replacing some words with abbreviations.**

You're a great designer! You should post pictures of your designs more often! I love them because they show feeling. Thanks for existing!

____

____

2 **Read these extracts from the forum discussion and answer the questions.**

AnnPaint says, "I would use a tablet and a stylus pen if I had access to them".

JoeCool2000 says, "If I had to make a portrait, I would stick to real art".

1 Does AnnPaint have access to a tablet and a stylus pen? No, she doesn't

2 Does JoeCool2000 have to make a portrait? No, he doesn't.

3 Are the sentences about real possibilities? Yes.

4 What time do the sentences refer to? Present, past or future? Future

5 How many clauses are there in the sentences? 1

6 Which elements do the sentences have in common? ______________

7 When is the comma used? ______________

Second Conditional

Second conditional sentences are used to refer to a **hypothesis**, an **unreal possibility**. They can refer to the present or the future.

If I **had** more time, I **would try** different techniques.

(I don't have more time, so I won't try different techniques.)

If I **were** you, I **would take** art lessons.

I **would take** art lessons if I **were** you.

3 **Read the dialogues below. Are they talking about a real (R) or an unreal (U) possibility?**

1 **Richard:** Are you going to visit any museums during your trip?

James: If I have time, I'll visit at least a history museum. R

Mariah: I can send you some suggestions if you want. R

2 **Mariah:** Are you going to visit any museums during your trip?

Dennis: My days are already fully booked. If I had more time, I'd visit at least one museum. U

Mariah: If I were you, I would try to do it. U

3 **Louise:** What will you do if your painting is selected for the exhibition? R

Beth: I guess I'll post it in all my social media if they allow me! R

Louise: If this happened to me, I'd do the same. U

4 **Look at the images and match them to the corresponding sentences. Then complete the sentences with the verb in parentheses in the correct form, using *would* or *wouldn't* when appropriate.**

1

2

3

a If Da Vinci was (be) so versatile, he would be (be) known for his incredible intelligence.

b If graffiti were (be) more recognized, people would saw (see) the brilliance behind it.

c He was (be) more interested in how The Parthenon was built if he would be (be) an architect.

5 **Look at activity 4 and complete the sentences below using your own ideas. Remember to use the second conditional.**

1 If I were as creative as Da Vinci, I would create. inv.

2 If I visited The Parthenon, I would spend hours.

3 If I met a famous graffiti artist, I would ask for an art.

Study Space

6 Complete the social media post with the verbs in parentheses in the correct form. You may also need to include *will* or *would* in some cases. Sometimes there is more than one possible answer.

Jane Irre

I'm not sure I get the difference between art and non-art. I know that if I (1) talk (talk) to people about it, everybody (2) will say (say) Da Vinci's paintings are art. I'm not a famous artist, but (3) would people consider (consider) my drawings art if I (4) posted (post) them without saying they are mine? And if my drawings (5) were (be) as good as Da Vinci's, (6) would I be (be) as famous as him?

7 Order the prompts to make questions. Add a comma when necessary.

1 you were invited / would / What / to a graffiti exhibition? / you do / if

What would you do if you were invited to a graffiti exhibition?

2 you think of it? / about graffiti / what / If / would / you knew very little

If you knew very little about graffiti what would you think of it?

3 if / Which actor or actress / the chance? / would / you had / you like to meet

Wich actor or actress would you like to meet if you had the chance?

4 beautiful building in your city / which one / it be? / choose the most / If you had to / would

If you had to choose the most beautiful building in your city wich one would it be.

5 you were taking part / where / would / If / in a selfie contest / you take your selfie?

If you were taking part

8 Answer the questions from activity 7 with information about yourself. Then interview a classmate and compare your answers.

1 ____________________

2 ____________________

3 ____________________

4 ____________________

9 Complete the sentences about architecture with your own ideas.

1 Architecture is super fun! If people studied more about it, ____________________.

2 If there weren't good architects, ____________________.

3 I really don't know anything about buildings. I would look at them differently if ____________________.

4 I don't care much about architecture, but I know I wouldn't live so comfortably if ____________________.

10 31 Listen to the opinion of four different people on architecture and write some keywords in your notebook. How similar are their opinions to your ideas from activity 9?

Pronunciation

11 32 Listen to the last sentence from activity 10 again and answer the questions.

I hate modern architecture! I can't **put up** with it. If it were that **good**, more people would **love** it!

1 Do the words in bold have the same vowel sound? ____________

2 Which of them are pronounced with /ʊ/, as in "book"? ____________

3 Which are pronounced with /ʌ/, as in "cup"? ____________

4 Can you think of other words with these sounds? ____________

12 33 Organize the words from the box in the chart. Then listen to the sentences and check your answers.

brush bush cut foot just look luck much pull push rug took

/ʊ/	/ʌ/

1 I need to buy a new brush for my Art class. I hope it doesn't cost too much.

2 This design museum has daily life objects with unexpected designs. My favorites are the rugs.

3 The new trend in my area is to cut bushes in the shape of animals.

4 He isn't that talented. His fame is just luck.

5 It took me some time to understand that painting. I had to look at it carefully.

6 The contemporary art museum has a new interactive installation. You can pull and push its parts to create new forms.

7 Have you watched that old movie about a boy who paints with his left foot?

13 34 Listen again and practice saying the sentences from activity 12.

Workbook p. 145

Study Space

WRITING

Writing Messages on an Online Forum

Before Writing

1 Plan your writing.

1. Choose a message on an online forum about a topic you are interested in.
2. Check if you have enough information to reply to the message appropriately.
3. Read all the messages that have already been written in the discussion thread.
4. Do you agree with these messages? Do you want to mention any of them in your own?
5. Take notes of the information you want to include in your message.

Drafting

2 Write a draft of your message.

3 Share your message with a classmate and ask for his/her opinion. Make adjustments, if necessary.

Final Writing

4 Write a final version of your message. Share it on #MAKERS Digital <www.richmondmakers.com>. Use the hashtag #OnlineForum.

INVESTIGATE

There are ____________ **art galleries** / **museums** / **movie theaters** in my town.

Collect Data

- Choose your focus: art galleries, museums or movie theaters. Circle it in the hypothesis sentence.
- Research the type of place you decided to investigate.
- Identify the number of places in your town and their characteristics.
- Find out if the places you found are specialized in a specific type of audience, e.g. children.

Type of Place	Number	Characteristics

Analyze the Data

- How many places did you expect to find in your research?
- How many places could you find?
- Are the places you found similar to each other?
- What makes the places different from each other?
- Are there more specialized places or more places dedicated to all types of audience?

Draw a Conclusion

There are ____________ **art galleries** / **museums** / **movie theaters** in my town.

1 Reflect on your conclusions and discuss.

1. Would you say that the number of places you found is big or small? Why?
2. In your opinion, what type of people would be interested in the places you found?
3. Did you find places for teenagers?
4. If so, do you go there? Why?
5. If not, what would make you want to go to this place?

2 Share your ideas on #MAKERS Digital <www.richmondmakers.com>. Use the hashtag #ArtInMyTown.

LOCAL AND GLOBAL

1 Look at the image of the painting *Starry Night*, by Vincent van Gogh. Do some research and complete the fact file about it.

WHERE WAS VINCENT VAN GOGH BORN?	
WHERE WAS HE WHEN HE PAINTED *STARRY NIGHT*?	
WHERE IS THE PAINTING *STARRY NIGHT* NOWADAYS?	

2 Research another work of art that was made in one country but is currently somewhere else. Fill in the fact file with information about it.

WHAT IS THE TITLE OF THE WORK OF ART?	
WHO MADE IT?	
WHERE WAS ITS CREATOR BORN?	
WHERE WAS HE/SHE WHEN HE/SHE MADE THIS WORK OF ART?	
WHERE IS THIS WORK OF ART NOWADAYS?	

3 Discuss the questions in groups.

1 How do works of art end up in countries other than the ones they were made in?

2 Who does a work of art belong to after its creator dies?

4 Find out if there are many international works of art in your country.

IMAGINE

Imagine looking like a painting.

1 Research into the concept. Bring your findings to be discussed in class.

2 Read the magazine article. Then discuss the questions with a classmate.

1 Would you like to have your portrait painted by an artist?

2 What does the app described in the article do?

3 Would you like to look like a famous painting?

4 Which style would you prefer your portrait to be painted in (realist, impressionist, cubist etc.)?

RTV

Makerspace p. 116

6

TO HAVE OR NOT TO HAVE

OBJECTIVES

- Identify gadgets, devices and appliances.
- Identify and talk about chores.
- Discuss the use of technology to do chores.
- Talk about life experiences.
- Use the words *yet*, *already*, *for* and *since* to talk about life experiences.
- Analyze, understand and produce an advertisement.
- Reflect on consumerism.

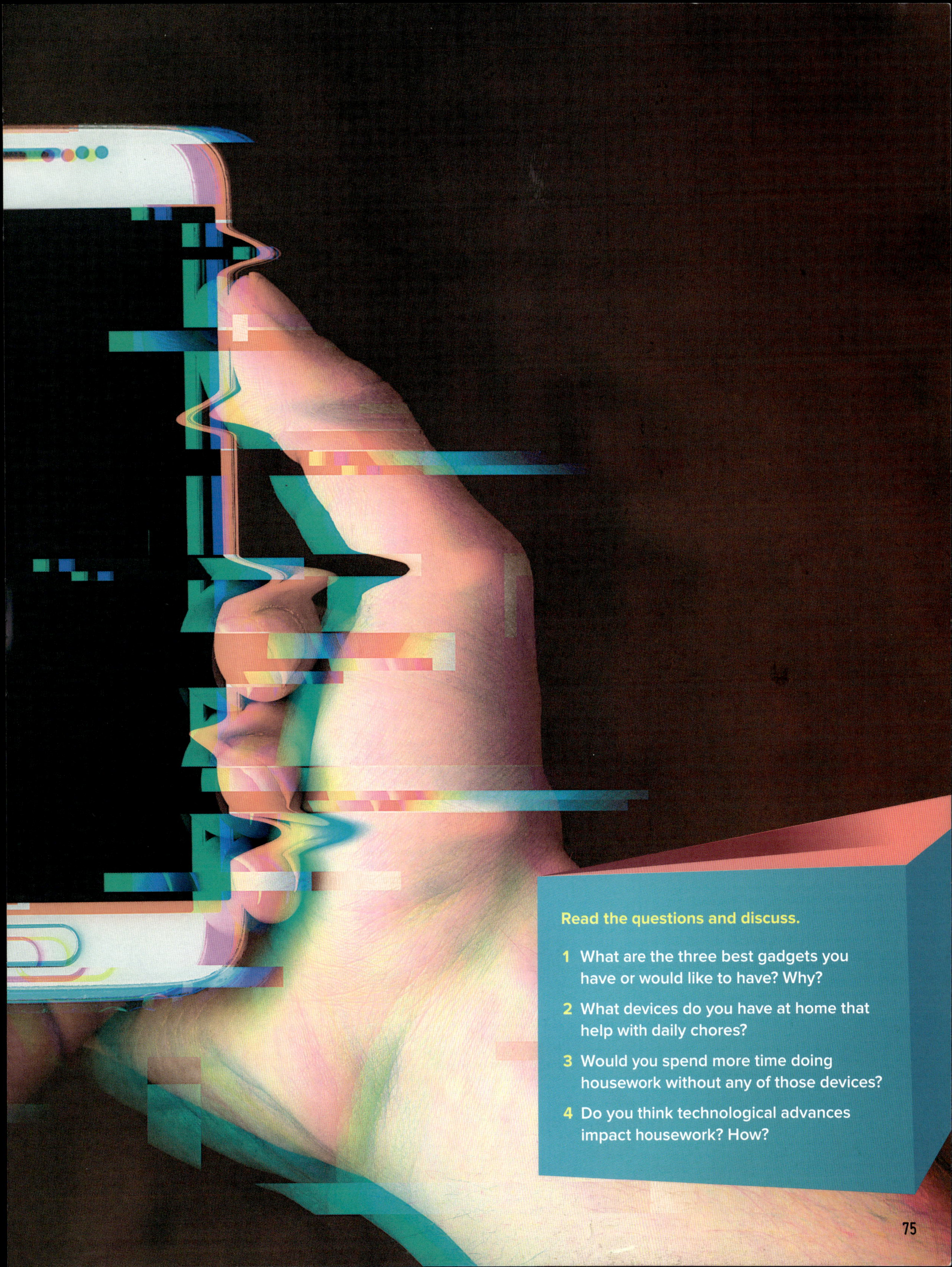

Read the questions and discuss.

1 What are the three best gadgets you have or would like to have? Why?

2 What devices do you have at home that help with daily chores?

3 Would you spend more time doing housework without any of those devices?

4 Do you think technological advances impact housework? How?

Richmond

#MAKERS DIGITAL

1

A dishwasher saves time, water and spares your hands.

2

Relax and let the robot vacuum do the cleaning.

3

The fastest way to heat food and drinks is by using a microwave oven.

4

You can keep track of your physical exercises with a smartwatch.

5

Use your smartphone to make payments, avoid long lines and save your time.

6

Smart washing machines let you manage your laundry via app.

RTV

1 **Look at the devices on page 76 and rank them from 1 (totally indispensable) to 6 (totally dispensable), according to your opinion.**

2 **In pairs, brainstorm some advantages and disadvantages of each device from page 76.**

3 35 **Listen to the podcast. Which of the devices from page 76 are not mentioned?**

4 36 **Listen again and match the devices with the corresponding disadvantages.**

1 microwave oven
2 dishwasher
3 washing machine
4 smartwatch

a ☐ uses a lot of water
b ☐ unsuitable for certain dishes
c ☐ unsuitable for certain types of food
d ☐ unsuitable for videos and long texts
e ☐ not affordable for everyone
f ☐ annoying frequent reminders
g ☐ noisy
h ☐ food gets cold too fast
i ☐ short battery life

5 **Are the disadvantages mentioned in the podcast similar to the ones you brainstormed in activity 2?**

6 **Discuss these questions with a classmate.**

1 Which of the devices mentioned in the audio does your family have? Which ones do they use most often? Why?
2 Some of those devices are quite expensive. Do you think they are worth the high price?

React!

7 **Read the discussion on the online forum below. Then write your own opinion.**

Are our devices making us lazy?

Samantha Jones Definitely! Before I had a smartphone to manage my life, I remembered details much more easily. I don't even write anything anymore, just type on my phone or computer—that's probably why my handwriting is almost illegible nowadays.

(1 day ago)

Eric Chang I don't think so… I guess lazy people don't need any excuses to do nothing all the time. Even if they don't have any devices, it doesn't mean they are less lazy. Besides, people who aren't usually lazy do much more with the help of technology instead of using it to produce less.

(2 days ago)

____

____

I Wonder

8 **Write a question about a device that you don't have, but would like to have. Then look for the answer.**

____

____

99 Great! 99 Interact

LANGUAGE 1

1 **Label the devices according to the words in the box.**

dishwasher iron
lawn mower microwave oven
refrigerator/fridge smartphone
smartwatch stove
vacuum cleaner washing machine

1 

2 

3 

4 

5 

6 

7 

8 

9 

10 

2 **Match the devices in activity 1 to the corresponding chores.**

a [ ] do the laundry
b [ ] keep food fresh
c [ ] cook
d [ ] do the dishes
e [1] pay bills
f [ ] defrost or heat food
g [ ] manage tasks
h [ ] vacuum
i [ ] mow the lawn
j [ ] iron clothes

Study Space My Glossary

3 **Complete the sentences either with the nouns from activity 1 or the verbs from activity 2.**

1 May I borrow your ____________, please? My dress got all wrinkled in the suitcase.

2 Can I wash my white clothes with yours? They're too few for a load in the ____________.

3 I was ____________, but I had to stop because it started to rain.

4 Have you seen the ad for that robot ____________? It's expensive, but I'm thinking of buying one. I simply can't stand vacuuming.

5 I don't know if I should ____________ or put them in the dishwasher.

4 **Read the ad below and complete it with words from activities 1 and 2. The first letter of each item is given.**

Do you think housekeeping chores are way too boring? Do you have a very busy life? If so, we have the perfect solution for you!

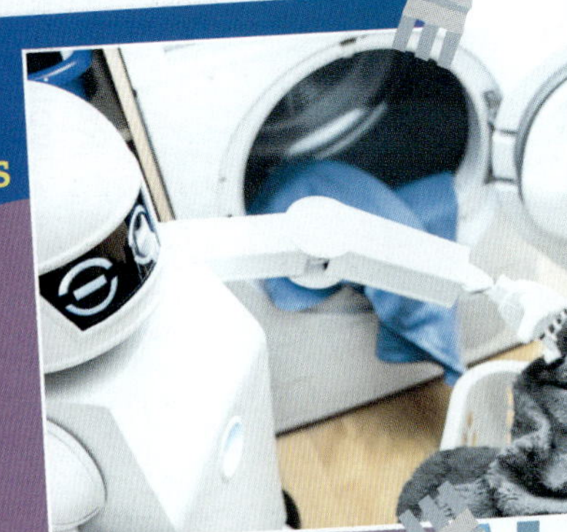

Most of us have more important or interesting activities to do than (1) v__________ or doing the (2) l__________, but we spend so much of our precious free time on housework that it feels like we don't have any free time at all.

ChoreTech is now making the old dream of substituting our several home devices for a single robot: with the brand new RobotikMaid 3000—the most complete housekeeping solution for all types of people and homes. Its advanced artificial intelligence system allows it to perform extremely complex tasks, such as (3) i__________ and (4) c__________. It can even use other appliances, including the (5) m__________ __________, the (6) d__________ and even the (7) l__________ __________. And you can program it via app to (8) m__________ __________ __________ according to your preferences. Just imagine... If you've already worked so hard all day long, get the rest you deserve and let the robot housekeeper do the hard work at home. Make it a reality with RobotikMaid 3000!

LISTENING AND SPEAKING

1 🎧37 **Listen to three extracts of a podcast and number the gadgets in the order they are mentioned.**

a ☐

b ☐
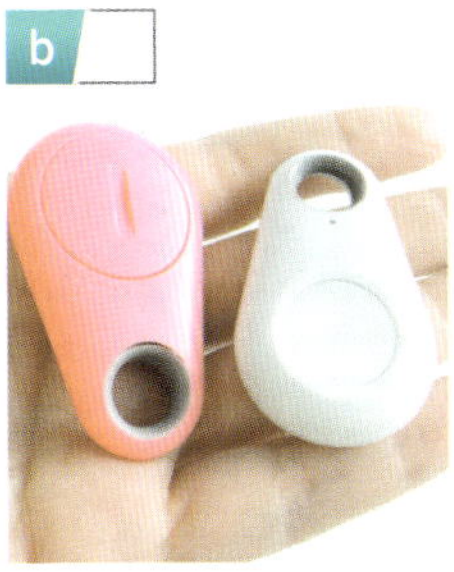
c ☐
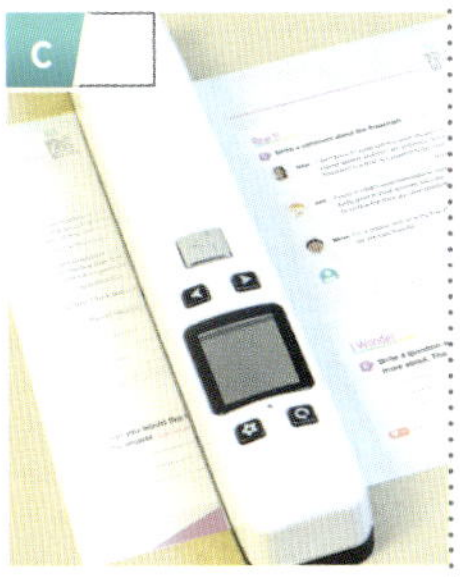

2 🎧38 **Listen to the extracts again and check the correct options.**

1 What is this podcast about?
   - a ☐ It's about gadgets for teachers to use in class.
   - b ☐ It's about useful gadgets for students.

2 According to the speaker, what's the easiest way to stay organized?
   - a ☐ To cut down on paper.
   - b ☐ To carry a lot of paper.

3 What can you do with a portable scanner?
   - a ☐ Organize files on your laptop.
   - b ☐ Scan papers and organize them digitally.

4 What advantages of an e-reader are mentioned?
   - a ☐ long battery life
   - b ☐ storage space for many books
   - c ☐ affordable
   - d ☐ lightweight design

5 Which objects were lost by the speaker?
   - a ☐ bike
   - b ☐ phone
   - c ☐ glasses
   - d ☐ umbrella
   - e ☐ car keys
   - f ☐ backpack

3 **Order the sequence of information as mentioned in the podcast.**

- a ☐ characteristics of the gadget (described with adjectives)
- b ☐ personal opinion/experience of the user
- c ☐ functions and ways to use the gadget

Buzzwords

"I can quickly scan my school notes ***on the fly****, organize them digitally and get rid of all the paper"*

What does "on the fly" mean? Look it up!

Pronunciation

4 🎧39 **Listen to the sentence below. How many syllables do you think the word in bold has?**

"I truly believe that cutting down on paper is the easiest way to get **organized**."

5 🎧40 **Say these words aloud and guess the corresponding number of syllables. Then listen and write them with separated syllables.**

because convenient
immediately organized space

- a 1 syllable: ____________________
- b 2 syllables: ____________________
- c 3 syllables: ____________________
- d 4 syllables: ____________________
- e 5 syllables: ____________________

6 **How is syllable separation in English different from the one in your language? Can you think of examples for comparison?**

7 **Discuss these questions in pairs.**

1 Which of the gadgets mentioned in activity 1 do you think is the most helpful for a student? Why?

2 What are some possible negative aspects of them?

3 What other gadgets can make a student's life easier? Give examples.

8 **Choose one of your own gadgets and describe it, following the sequence from activity 3.**

9 **Based on your description, make a presentation about your gadget to a classmate.**

10 **Record your presentation and share it on #MAKERS Digital <www.richmondmakers.com> using the hashtag #MyGadget.**

Makerspace p. 117 Study Space

READING

Before Reading

1 Scan the texts and answer the questions.

1. What kind of texts are these? ______________________________
2. Where can you find texts like these? ______________________________
3. What is the main objective of this kind of text? ______________________________
4. Who usually produces texts like these? ______________________________

2 Classify the elements of the texts as V (verbal), NV (nonverbal) or B (both).

1. [ ] style of language (sophisticated, technical, informal etc.)
2. [ ] colors
3. [ ] distribution and position of elements
4. [ ] typography (unique font type, font size etc.)
5. [ ] humor
6. [ ] creativity
7. [ ] interactivity

While Reading

3 **The elements in the box are usually found in ads. Write them next to their definition. Then read the ads in activity 1 and check the elements that appear in them.**

background image
brand logo brand name
call to action contact information
main text product image
product name slogan title

1 ☐ word or short phrase that introduces the topic of the ad: ____________
2 ☐ name by which a company is known: ____________
3 ☐ information for consumers to communicate and interact with a company: ____________
4 ☐ photo or illustration of the specific product being advertised: ____________
5 ☐ a short phrase that is easy to remember and to relate to a brand: ____________
6 ☐ scenery, people, objects, shapes and other items that form a context for the ad: ____________
7 ☐ a symbol that represents a company: ____________
8 ☐ a phrase to make the consumer do something that will lead to him/her buying the product: ____________
9 ☐ information that connects all the other elements in an ad to generate interest: ____________
10 ☐ name a company gives to a specific product: ____________

4 **Ads aim to convince the customer of the benefits of purchasing something. Read the benefits below and write the name of the product related to each.**

1 finding lost objects: ________
2 spending less time on housework: ________
3 keeping your schedule updated: ________
4 not worrying about losing important things: ________
5 feeling happy because you have completed your tasks: ________
6 keeping floors clean: ________
7 not forgetting what you have to do: ________

5 **Read the ads again and match them to their target audiences.**

a ☐ Teenagers, young adults and adults; any gender; lower-middle to upper social classes; students, professionals and busy people, especially those who often deal with deadlines.

b ☐ Adults in their 20s or older; any gender; middle to upper social classes; professionals and busy people, especially those who work and live by themselves and who feel comfortable around technology.

c ☐ Teenagers, young adults and adults; any gender; middle to upper social classes; busy and forgetful people who feel comfortable around technology.

6 **Is it important to have the target audience in mind when writing an ad? Why?**

____
____
____
____

After Reading

7 **Choose one of the products below and advertise it to a new target audience.**

1 AutoVak / adults who feel comfortable around technology
2 Track'Em / children who have many toys
3 List.do.it / elderly who have started using a smartphone

8 **Discuss these questions with a classmate.**

1 How do the ads in activity 1 make you feel? Would you consider buying the products? Why?
2 Ads only present the advantages of the product and sometimes exaggerate them or omit important disadvantages. Can you think of any "hidden issues" in the ads? If so, what are they? Would they impact on your decision when thinking of buying the products?
3 In your opinion, how much can advertisements actually influence people to buying products?
4 Do you think it is important to be aware of that influence? If so, how can we become more aware of it?

Study Space Workbook p. 147

LANGUAGE 2

1 Analyze the words in bold. Underline the auxiliary verbs and circle the main verbs.

1 **Have** you **cleaned** your carpets?

2 Her allergy **has gotten** worse.

3 Let's see if there's any task I **haven't finished** yet.

Present Perfect

Affirmative

I/You/We/They**'ve/have won** a prize.
He/She/It**'s/has arrived** in town.

Negative

I/You/We/They **haven't/have not found** a house.
He/She/It **hasn't/has not woken up**.

Interrogative

Have I/you/we/they **bought** the tickets?
Has he/she/it **slept** on the couch?

Short Answers

Yes, I/you/we/they **have**. / No, I/you/we/they **haven't**.
Yes, he/she/it **has**. / No, he/she/it **hasn't**.

The **present perfect** can be used to...

- talk about actions that happened in the past but have an effect in the present.
  I **have lost** my phone. (I don't have it now.)
- describe actions and situations that started in the past and continue into the present.
  Grandma's allergy **has gotten** worse since spring started.
- talk about life experiences.
  My brother **has visited** five different countries.

2 Read Lilly and Rick's conversation. Then complete it with the present perfect of the verbs in parentheses.

Rick: Hi, Lilly! You look worried. (1) ________ anything ________ (happen)?

Lilly: Hey! No, not really. It's just that I was talking to Grandma and Grandpa this morning and it got me thinking about life. Did you know that they (2) __________ (do) lots of amazing things?

Rick: Really? I had no idea! I (3) ________________ (have – neg.) a conversation with them for a while, actually. I guess I should pay them a visit.

Lilly: You definitely should! Grandma told me she (4) ________ (move) more than 10 times. She (5) ________ (meet) a lot of different people too. Some of them (6) ________ (be) her close friends for over 30 years now.

3 41 Listen to the questions and check the correct answers.

1 a ☐ No, I haven't.
  b ☐ I have had a breakfast.

2 a ☐ Yes, she has.
  b ☐ She has been there many times.

3 a ☐ I've never eaten insects.
  b ☐ I've eaten insects once.

4 a ☐ Yes, he has read it.
  b ☐ He's read it twice.

4 Read the ads on page 80 again and analyze the use of the words *already*, *for*, *since* and *yet*. Then circle the correct options.

1 Use ***already*** / ***yet*** in affirmative sentences to talk about an action that happened sooner than expected.

2 Use ***already*** / ***yet*** in negative sentences to talk about something that has not happened, but will probably happen soon.

3 Use ***already*** / ***yet*** in questions to ask about events that are expected to have happened or to happen soon.

4 Use ***for*** / ***since*** to determine a moment when something started.

5 Use ***for*** / ***since*** to determine a period of time.

Adverbs *already, yet, for, since*

Use ***already*** in affirmative sentences about an action/event that happened sooner than expected.
My brother has **already** finished his homework for today and it's still 3 p.m.!

Use ***yet*** in negative sentences about an action/event that has not happened.
I haven't finished the assignment **yet**. I still have three pages to write.

Use ***yet*** in interrogative sentences about an action/event that is expected to have happened or to happen soon.
A: Have you read it **yet**?
B: Not yet. I'll do it in 5 minutes.

Use ***since*** to talk about a moment when an action/event started.
She's studied English **since** 2015.

Use ***for*** to talk about a period of time.
We've known each other **for** 2 years.

Study Space

5 Complete the chart with the expressions from the box.

9 o'clock a few weeks now a long time
a while I was 10 January last night
my birthday seven years twenty minutes

for	since

6 Complete the sentences with *already*, *yet*, *for* or *since*.

1

Has it stopped raining ______?

2

I'm starving! I haven't eaten anything ______ breakfast.

3

I've ______ paid all of this month's bills.

4

I haven't seen my friends ______ our vacation started.

5

I've had these sneakers ______ a very long time. They're really worn out.

6

I haven't done the History assignment ______, but it's due tomorrow.

7 Write replies using the present perfect and the prompts.

1 **A:** Come on, Sam. Get a plate and help yourself.
B: Thanks, but I've already had lunch. (already)

2 **A:** Have you heard about what happened in Japan?
B: ______________________ (yet)

3 **A:** Can you play the piano?
B: ______________________ (for)

4 **A:** Have you seen Thomas today?
B: ______________________ (already)

5 **A:** Hey! I didn't know you wore glasses.
B: ______________________ (since)

6 **A:** Has Mark been to the doctor this month?
B: ______________________ (yet)

8 Complete the sentences with true information about you.

1 I've already ____________ this week.
2 I haven't ____________ yet.
3 I have ____________ for a long time.
4 I haven't ____________ for about two weeks.
5 I have ____________ since I was a child.
6 I haven't ____________ since last year.

9 Transform the sentences in activity 8 into questions and ask them to a classmate. Take notes on his/her answers.

A: Have you done the Math homework this week yet?
B: Yes, I have.

10 Answer the questions with true information about yourself.

1 Have you eaten anything yet?
____

2 Have you finished all your assignments for this week?
____

3 Have you done any chores at home since last Sunday?
____

4 Have you used your smartphone in the last 30 minutes?
____

5 Have you taken notes in class this week?
____

Workbook p. 147

WRITING

An Advertisement

Before Writing

1 Consider the following to plan your ad.

1 Take a look at pages 80 and 81 and choose 5 elements and/or aspects of advertisements that you consider the most important.

2 Choose a gadget for your ad—it must be a device that you have used at least once.

3 Research and take notes on at least 3 advantages and/or special features of the gadget you have chosen.

4 Define the target audience.

5 List a few keywords you can use in your ad. If necessary, use a dictionary to find more interesting synonyms.

6 Decide on the images you are going to use and how the different elements (verbal and nonverbal) are going to be positioned in your ad.

Drafting

2 Make a draft of your ad. If you don't have an image yet, write a brief description of it.

3 Share your ad with a classmate and ask for his/her opinion. Make adjustments, if necessary.

Final Writing

4 Write the final version of your ad and post it on #MAKERS Digital <www.richmondmakers.com>. Use the hashtag **#MyAd**.

INVESTIGATE

a few a lot almost all

I use gadgets and devices to do ____________ of my chores on a typical day.

Collect Data

- Pay attention to and take notes of all your daily chores for three days.
- Repeat the chore as many times as necessary.
- Indicate whether any tools/devices were used to do it. If so, name them.

Analyze the Data

- Which chores do you do more frequently?
- Are your chores simple or more complex?
- Do you do them at home or somewhere else?
- Do you do them alone or in collaboration with others?
- For what percentage of the chores do you use any tools/devices?
- For what percentage of the chores do you use some kind of technology?
- What percentage of the chores actually requires the use of technology?

Draw a Conclusion

I use gadgets and devices to do ____________ of my chores on a typical day.

1 Reflect on the conclusion and discuss in pairs.

1 Do you and your classmate do the same chores? If not, how do the differences impact on the use of technology?

2 Do you and your classmate use technology for the same chores?

3 Do you think you and/or your classmate are dependent on technology to do the chores?

4 Would it be easy or difficult to reduce your use of technology? Why?

2 Share your ideas on #MAKERS Digital <www.richmondmakers.com>. Use the hashtag **#GadgetsAndChores**.

LOCAL AND GLOBAL

1 Look at the images and discuss the questions with a classmate.

interactive whiteboard

computers

virtual reality headsets

robotics

1 Are any of these devices available at your school? If so, how often do you use them?

2 What educational benefits do you think they can offer?

3 In your opinion, which device(s) can impact the most on the learning process? Why?

4 Do you think the lack of technology in schools can affect students' development? If so, how?

2 Research the availability and usage of education technology in the city, state and country where you live. Use these questions as a guide and take notes on your findings.

1 What is the percentage of schools that have a computer lab or computers in the classroom?

2 What is the percentage of schools that have internet access?

3 Are there any public incentives for education technology? If so, what is the percentage of schools that receive them?

4 Are there any public programs for implementing education technology and training school staff? If so, what is the percentage of schools that participate in them?

3 Compare your findings from activity 2 with a classmate and discuss these questions.

1 What are the positive and negative aspects of the use of technology where you live?

2 Is there anything that could be improved? If so, what and how?

IMAGINE

Imagine making your home totally smart.

1 Research into the concept. Bring your research to be discussed in class.

2 Read the text. Then discuss with a classmate.

1 What negative aspects of having a smart home are mentioned in the text?

2 Do you agree with the perspectives expressed by the author? Why?

RTV

REVIEW 5

1 **Write questions for the answers below using the words given. Then answer them with information about yourself.**

1 (fond) ______________________________

I don't like European cinema very much. I prefer American movies.

____

2 (famous) ______________________________

I'd like to be known for my drawings.

____

3 (good) ______________________________

If I could choose, I'd like to be a talented designer.

____

4 (interested) ______________________________

I'm not sure, but I like photography.

____

5 (excited) ______________________________

I'm really into visual arts, but I have no talent to become an artist.

____

2 **Use the questions in activity 1 to interview a classmate.**

3 **Complete the blanks using the correct form of the verbs in parentheses. Then continue the sentences with your own ideas.**

1 If Pablo Picasso __________ (be) alive nowadays, ______________________________.

2 We __________ (cancel) the exhibition if ______________________________.

3 He __________ (paint) whatever you wanted if ______________________________.

4 If Phillip __________ (know) more about digital art, he ______________________________.

5 If Carol __________ (not take) photography classes regularly, ______________________________.

4 42 **Listen to Melany talking about her talent and her studies. Take notes about her situation. What would you do if you were her?**

____

____

____

____

5 **Speculate about how things would be if the following statements weren't true. Make the necessary changes to the original ones.**

1 Graffiti isn't so popular in my city. Our walls are boring.

If graffiti were more popular in my city, our walls wouldn't be so boring.

2 You aren't interested in architecture. You don't know how modern the buildings in Tokyo are.

____

____

3 You don't watch classic movies. You don't notice their influence on modern cinema.

____

____

4 You aren't good at taking pictures. We have to pay a professional photographer.

____

____

5 You never read about Surrealism. You don't understand Salvador Dalí's paintings.

____

____

6 **Complete the questions based on the images.**

1

What would you do if ______________________________?

2

What material would you use if ______________________________?

3

If you could meet any famous person, ______________________________?

4

Who would you photograph if ______________________________?

7 **Use your questions from activity 6 to interview your classmates.**

REVIEW 6

1 Look at the images and write the names of the devices you see in each room.

1 bedroom: ____________, ____________.

2 kitchen: ____________, ____________, ____________, ____________.

3 laundry room: ____________, ____________, ____________.

2 Complete the answers in the dialogues with the present perfect of the appropriate verbs and *since* or *for*.

1 **A:** Steve is still on vacation, isn't he?
B: Yes. He ____________ on vacation ____________ last week.

2 **A:** Do you see Sue every day?
B: No. Actually, I ____________ her ____________ at least a month.

3 **A:** Do you like to watch TV?
B: Not really. I ____________ TV ____________ ages.

4 **A:** Do you know Laura?
B: Sure. We ____________ each other ____________ we were children.

5 **A:** Would you like to have some coffee?
B: No, thanks. I ____________ (already) three cups ____________ I arrived.

3 Read the sentences below. Then check the ones that are right and correct the ones that are wrong.

1 ☑ My parents have been married for 15 years.
____

2 ☐ I've studied at the same school in 2013.
____

3 ☐ Jessica's been a vegetarian since she was 14.
____

4 ☐ We hasn't vacuumed here for weeks now... since the vacuum cleaner broke.
____

4 This is the Smiths' chore chart for this week. Consider that today is Wednesday and write complete answers using *already* or *yet*.

	Mon	Tue	Wed	Thu	Fri
Mrs. Smith	cook 👍	do the laundry 👍	clean the kitchen 👍	clean the living room	pay the bills
Mr. Smith	do the dishes 👍	clean the bathroom 👍	cook 👍	take out the trash	clean the kitchen
Julia	take out the trash 👍	water the plants 👍	do the dishes 👍	iron clothes	cook
James	clean the kitchen 👍	vacuum 👍	clean the bedrooms 👍	clean the bathroom	mow the lawn

1 Has Mr. Smith cooked yet?
Yes, he has. He's already cooked.

2 Has Mrs. Smith cleaned the living room yet?
No, she hasn't. She hasn't cleaned the living room yet.

3 Have the Smiths ironed clothes yet?
____

4 Has Julia done the dishes yet?
____

5 Has Mrs. Smith done the laundry yet?
____

6 Has James vacuumed yet?
____

7 Has Mrs. Smith cleaned the kitchen yet?
____

8 Has James mowed the lawn yet?
____

7

HANDLING CONFLICT

OBJECTIVES

- Learn and talk about different types of conflict.
- Listen to people talking about conflicts and discuss the topic.
- Read about refugees and what they carry with them.
- Talk about different types of past experiences.
- Ask for confirmation and agreement.
- Investigate the most common themes of photo-essays.
- Make a photo-essay.
- Reflect on what makes a city dangerous and what can be done to make it safer.
- Reflect on potential benefits of conflicts.

Read the questions and discuss.

1 What do you think the opening image of the unit represents?

2 What types of conflict can you think of?

3 What conflicts are going on around the world right now?

4 How is it possible to end a conflict?

Richmond

#MAKERS DIGITAL

1 "TREAT YOUR FRIENDS LIKE YOU DO YOUR BEST PICTURES; PLACE THEM IN THE BEST LIGHT."

UNKNOWN

At the spur of the moment, we may not find the right words and end up being misunderstood and hurting people's feelings. Here are a few tips to avoid that:

1. Do you need to talk about it now? Sometimes, it's better to calm down before talking about something that upsets you.
2. Breathe and focus. Try not to let your emotions get the best of you.
3. Listen more than you talk. A Chinese proverb says, "We have two ears and one mouth, so that we can listen twice as much as we speak.".
4. Focus on what the other person is trying to say. Emotions may also prevent them from being clear.
5. Put yourself in the other person's shoes. Make an effort to understand how they are feeling.
6. Consider the consequences. Remember that a conflict may bring some negative results. Have in mind a course of action, in case this happens.

Based on <https://tinybuddha.com/blog/conflicts-with-friends-13-ways-to-communicate-without-drama/>. Accessed on July 20, 2018.

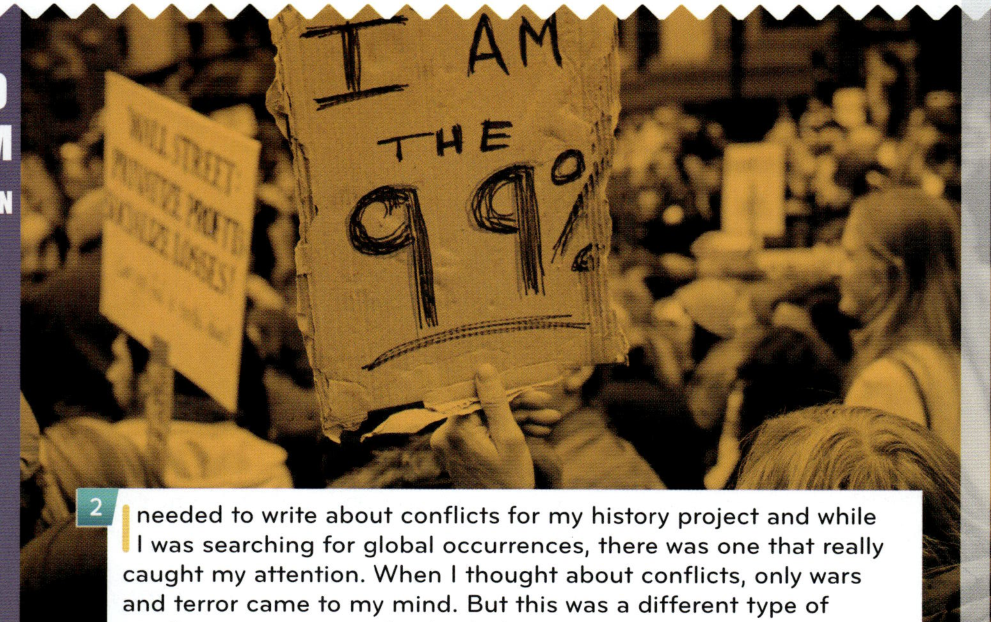

2

I needed to write about conflicts for my history project and while I was searching for global occurrences, there was one that really caught my attention. When I thought about conflicts, only wars and terror came to my mind. But this was a different type of conflict—it was a popular, leaderless resistance movement.

In their own words, Occupy Wall Street was made of people of different colors, genders and political views. They saw themselves as the 99% of the population that wanted to end the greed and corruption of the 1%. Their massive demonstrations were marked by nonviolence.

The movement started with the occupation of Zuccotti Park, in New York, in September 2011. In November of the same year, people were forced to leave the park, but they generated a wave of demonstrations all over the world.

Based on <http://occupywallst.org/>. Accessed on July 23, 2018.

RTV

1 43 **Listen to a psychologist talking. Then read the magazine article and the blog post. What do the texts have in common?**

a ☐ They are about people in conflict areas.

b ☐ They are about different types of conflicts.

c ☐ They are about how people feel in a conflict.

2 **Match the titles to the texts on page 90.**

a ☐ We Are the 99%

b ☐ 6 Tips to Communicate Effectively During a Conflict

3 **Explain the following quotes in your own words.**

1 "Your worst battle is between what you know and what you feel."

2 "Treat your friends like you do your best pictures; place them in the best light."

4 **Find the Chinese proverb in the texts. Then discuss the following questions with a classmate.**

1 Have you ever heard this proverb?

2 Do you agree with the message in it? Why?

3 Is there a similar proverb in your language? If so, does it mean the same?

4 Do you think you listen more than you speak? Why?

5 Do you agree that this is a good way to resolve conflicts? Why?

React!

5 **What type of conflict worries you the most? Write a comment about it.**

Allyah_Mendez International conflicts are the ones that worry me the most because they can start wars!

Paul_York Well, it's hard to say. But I think the ones that are close to me are the worst. In my city, for example, street gangs fight over power and that scares me a lot!

Corina_Strauss I guess everyday-life conflicts worry me the most. I hate it when I see families arguing. It's heartbreaking!

GamerBoy Conflicts don't worry me much, to be honest. They're a natural part of life and they're necessary so that there's change.

I Wonder

6 **Write a question about conflicts. Then look for the answer.**

99 Great! 99 Interact

LANGUAGE 1

1 Read the sentences. Are the words in bold nouns or verbs?

6 Tips to **Communicate** Effectively During a Conflict

Consider the consequences.

Emotions may also **prevent** them from being clear.

2 Complete the chart.

Noun	Verb
argument	argue
communication	
	consider
prevention	
	resolve

3 Rewrite the sentences using the verbs from the box. Make any necessary changes. Follow the example.

argue ~~communicate~~ consider prevent resolve

1 There should be better communication between governments.
Governments should communicate better.

2 People must take into consideration the two sides of a story.

____

3 It's no use having an argument over that topic.

____

4 The solution to some conflicts is the prevention of corruption.

____

5 He had a great idea for the resolution of the problem.

____

Study Space

4 Check the correct options to complete the following comments in an online forum. Use a dictionary if necessary.

fake news

SnowFlake
Today, most people are willing to (1) ______ and avoid misunderstandings. There are many campaigns to (2) ______ the spread of fake news and people are being encouraged to (3) ______ the impact of what they share on the internet.

a ◯ prevent, communicate, consider
b ◯ communicate, prevent, consider
c ◯ consider, prevent, communicate

FireFlame
@SnowFlake This is so necessary! People sometimes (4) ______ because of fake news and it's hard to (5) ______ this type of conflict!

a ◯ argue, resolve
b ◯ resolve, argue

5 Match the two parts of the expressions. Then use them to complete the sentences.

1 have — a ☐ a commitment
2 take — b ☐ a course of action
3 suggest — c ☐ a misunderstanding
4 make — d ☐ responsibility
5 accept — e ☐ your apology

1 I think we ______________ about the project. Let's review it together.

2 People should ______________ for their actions and understand that there might be consequences.

3 If you're familiar with the problem, please ______________.

4 It's easier to ______________ when we have clear goals.

5 I see your point. That's fine, I ______________.

6 Write sentences about yourself using the expressions from activity 5.

1 ______________________________
2 ______________________________
3 ______________________________
4 ______________________________
5 ______________________________

My Glossary

LISTENING AND SPEAKING

1 44 **Listen to a conversation between some teenagers and check the type of party they are planning.**

1 ☐

A sweet sixteen party.

2 ☐

A prom.

3 ☐

A pool party.

2 45 **Order the events as they happen. Then listen to the conversation again and check your answers.**

a ☐ Jack says he does not know where to get a mask.

b ☐ Amber asks Nicole and Jack for ideas for the event they are organizing.

c ☐ Everyone comes to an agreement.

d ☐ Nicole and Jack criticize each other's ideas.

e ☐ Amber suggests that they join both ideas.

f ☐ Nicole suggests that they customize their masks in the art class.

g ☐ Nicole and Jack suggest ideas.

3 **Answer the questions according to the conversation.**

1 What are the themes suggested for the prom?

2 Why doesn't Nicole like Jack's suggestion?

3 Why isn't Jack happy about the idea of the mask?

4 What type of conflict is there in the conversation?

5 How do Jack and Nicole come to an agreement?

4 **Do you think the conflict was resolved in a good way? Why?**

5 **Have you ever experienced a situation in which you had to resolve a conflict? What did you do?**

Buzzwords

"I'm ***fed up with*** *people dressed as celebrities."*

What does "fed up with" mean? Look it up!

6 **What are you fed up with? Make a list and tell a classmate.**

1

2

3

7 **Imagine you are going to resolve a conflict between two friends. Follow the instructions.**

1 Get together in trios.

2 Set the theme you are going to discuss.

3 Two students should have opposite points of view. The third one is going to mediate the conflict.

4 Solve the conflict.

8 **Record your course of action and share it on #MAKERS Digital <www.richmondmakers.com>. Use the hashtag #ConflictResolution.**

Study Space

READING

Before Reading

1 Read the title of the text. What's in your bag right now?

https://medium.com/uprooted/what-s-in-my-bag-758d435f6e62

WHAT'S IN MY BAG?

WHAT REFUGEES BRING WHEN THEY RUN FOR THEIR LIVES

In 2015, nearly 100,000 men, women and children from war-torn countries in the Middle East, North Africa and South Asia fled their homes and traveled by rubber dinghies across the Aegean Sea to Greece.

Refugees travel light, for their trek is arduous. Smugglers routinely exploit them, promising safety for a price, only to squeeze them like sardines into tiny boats. Most have no option but to shed whatever meager belongings they may have salvaged from their journeys.

The International Rescue Committee asked a mother, a child and a teenager to show us what they managed to hold on to from their homes. Their possessions tell stories about their past and their hopes for the future.

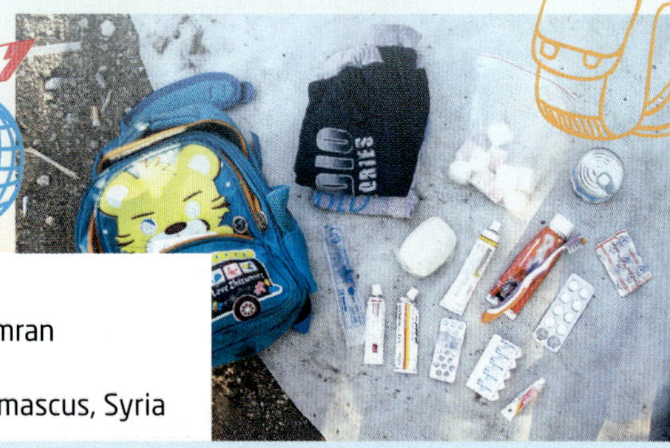

A Child

Name: Omran
Age: 6
From: Damascus, Syria

Little Omran, wearing a cheerful blue shirt, is on his way to Germany with his extended family of five to live with relatives. Because his parents knew they would travel through forests to avoid detection, they made sure to pack bandages for scrapes and cuts.

A Mother

Name: Aboessa*
Age: 20
From: Damascus, Syria

When vicious fighting erupted in Yarmouk, an unofficial camp for Palestinians just south of the Syrian capital, Aboessa managed to escape with her husband and their 10-month-old daughter, Doua. After crossing the border to Turkey, they spent one week sheltering in a forlorn camp before jumping into a rubber raft bound for the safe shores of Europe.

The Turkish police patrolling the coast stopped them and detached the boat's motor in order to force them to turn back, but the refugees kept going, steering the boat through the sea's strong currents with paddles they made.

"Everything is for my daughter, to protect her against sickness. When we arrived in Greece, a kind man gave me two jars of food. Another man gave us biscuits and water when he saw my baby."

A Teenager

Name: Iqbal
Age: 17
From: Kunduz, Afghanistan

Iqbal dragged his exhausted body out of the boat with only a backpack. The teenager traveled hundreds of miles and dodged bullets to escape from the warring province of Kunduz in northern Afghanistan, fleeing east to Iran, then traveling by foot to Turkey. Now in Greece, he's uncertain of where to go next. He has kept in touch with a friend who already made the journey to Germany. He also has a brother studying in Florida.

"I want my skin to be white and my hair to be spiked—I don't want them to know I'm a refugee, do I? I think that someone will spot me and call the police because I'm illegal."

*Last names omitted to protect the privacy of those interviewed.

Photos by Tyler Jump; Produced by Kulsoom Rizvi

Adapted from <https://medium.com/uprooted/what-s-in-my-bag-758d435f6e62>. Accessed on July 24, 2018.

2 **Look at the text and check the correct options.**

1 What elements can you see?

a ☐ Graphs and charts.

b ☐ Images and short texts.

2 What type of text is this?

a ☐ A photo-essay.

b ☐ A newspaper article.

3 **What do you think the text is about, by looking at the images and the title?**

1 ☐ People's lost items while traveling to another country.

2 ☐ People's belongings when they leave their countries.

3 ☐ People's favorite items.

4 **Why do you think images are used in this type of text?**

______

______

______

______

While Reading

5 **Answer the questions according to the photo-essay.**

1 What do the people mentioned have in common?

______

2 Who put their stories together?

______

3 Why do these people carry few things with them?

______

4 Where are the people from?

______

5 What can people's bags tell us about them?

______

6 **Write the name of the person who is in each situation.**

1 Germany and Florida are possible destinations for this person. ______

2 Kind people gave food to this person's family. ______

3 This person had to travel through the forest to avoid being caught. ______

7 **Look at the items each person could bring. Can you see any similarities? Follow the example.**

1 They all have tooth paste.

2 ______

3 ______

4 ______

5 ______

8 **Find the words in the text that mean the following. Use a dictionary, if necessary.**

1 Small boats used for recreation or racing. ______

2 A long walk. ______

3 A person that takes people to or from a country illegally. ______

4 Get rid of things you can't take with you. ______

5 Deserted. ______

9 **Read the text again and find evidence of the following.**

1 Aboessa is worried about her daughter.

______

2 People had empathy for Aboessa's daughter.

______

3 Iqbal is worried about his appearance.

______

4 Iqbal thinks people don't like refugees.

______

Study Space

After Reading

10 **What items would you bring with you if you had to leave your home abruptly?**

11 **Reflect on these questions and share your opinions with a classmate.**

1 What types of conflict force people to run away from their countries?

2 What are the difficulties that refugees face?

3 How are refugees usually treated by people when they get to a new country?

4 How do refugees feel when they arrive in a new country?

5 What policies are there in your country to help refugees?

Workbook p. 149

LANGUAGE 2

1 These sentences were taken from the photo-essay on page 94. Read them and answer the questions.

1 When we arrived in Greece, a kind man gave me two jars of food.

2 He has kept in touch with a friend who already made the journey to Germany.

a Which sentence uses the present perfect? ______

b Which sentence uses the simple past? ______

Present Perfect vs. Simple Past

The **present perfect** is used to talk about actions that started in the past and continue up to the present or that impact the present. It is also used to talk about the number of times something was done.
We usually use ***already***, ***ever***, ***never***, ***for***, ***since*** and ***yet*** with the present perfect.

The **simple past** is used to talk about actions that started and finished in the past. We usually use time expressions like ***last week***, ***yesterday***, ***two days ago*** etc. with the simple past.

Study Space

2 Circle the correct option to complete each sentence.

1 I **have known** / **knew** her since she arrived here.

2 He **saw** / **has seen** his father last year.

3 Kaleb **already read** / **has already read** all the information about adopting a refugee child.

4 Sally **has had** / **had** a strange dream last night.

5 Yesterday, my parents **rescued** / **have rescued** a stray dog.

6 Sabrina **built** / **has built** a tree house for her family. Look at it, so pretty!

Snack Learning

I have **(already)** been to Istanbul.
I haven't been to Istanbul **(yet)**.
Have you **(ever)** been to Istanbul?
Yes, I have. / No, I haven't.

3 Will is driving a passenger to the airport. Complete their conversation with the verbs from the box in the correct tense.

be (2x) have live see (2x)

Will: Good morning!

Arav: Good morning! To the airport, please. Oh, I can't believe I'm going to see my parents again!

Will: May I ask where you're from, sir?

Arav: I'm from India. But I (1) ______ here in Australia for 10 years. (2) ______ you ______ to India?

Will: No, I (3) ______. But I would like to! When (4) ______ the last time you (5) ______ your parents?

Arav: I (6) ______ them since 2015.

Will: Wow! That's a long time!

Arav: Yes, it is! But now they're coming to spend a whole month with me! I'm very happy!

4 Write true sentences about yourself using the prompts and the appropriate verb tenses.

1 for: ______

2 already: ______

3 last year: ______

4 never: ______

5 two days ago: ______

5 Write questions to complete the radio interview.

Paul: We're here with Melina Callas, from the "Make Friends, Not War" movement. Welcome, Melina!

Melina: Thank you, Paul.

Paul: Can you explain to us what this movement's about?

Melina: Sure. It's about making friends with refugee young people. We show them around the city and make them feel at home.

Paul: And why (1) ______?

Melina: I started this movement because I saw a documentary about the difficulties faced by refugees and wanted to help.

Paul: And how many (2) ______?

Melina: I think we've helped around 200 people.

Paul: Fantastic! And what (3) ______?

Melina: What I've learned from this experience is that we don't need much to be happy. And we can always start over.

Paul: I see... Thank you so much, Melina! And good luck!

6 Read the sentence. What is the objective of the question in bold?

I don't want them to know
I'm a refugee, **do I?**

____

7 Circle all the options that apply.

About the sentence in activity 6, it is correct to say that...

a the question comes at the end of the sentence.
b both the sentence and the question are in the negative.
c the sentence is in the negative, but the question is in the affirmative.
d the sentence and the question are in the same tense.

Tag Questions

Tag questions are short questions used at the end of sentences, especially in spoken English. They are mostly used to ask for confirmation or agreement.

Snack Learning

I am wrong, **aren't I?**
Let's go to the movies, **shall we?**
Please take this book back to the library for me, **will you?**

Study Space

8 Two friends are talking about helping refugees. Complete their conversations with tag questions.

Gabby: You haven't seen that new documentary about refugees, (1) ________

Ariel: Actually, I have! It's great, (2) ________

Gabby: It is! I feel I should do something about it. You don't know any organizations that help refugees, (3) ________

Ariel: I don't... But Sally helps an NGO, (4) ________

Gabby: She does! Let's talk to her, (5) ________

9 Write tag questions using the images and the prompts.

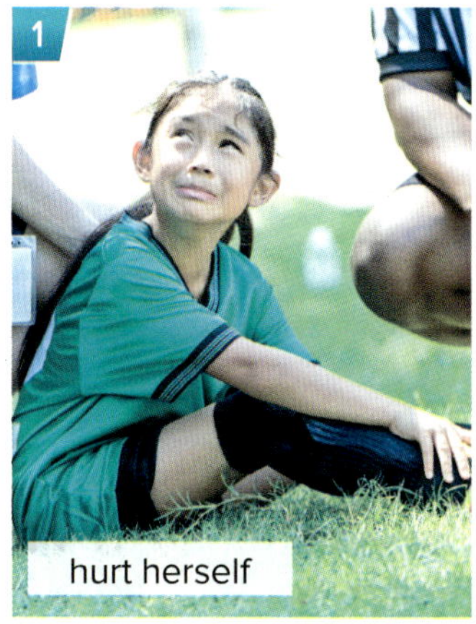

____

Pronunciation

10 46 Listen to the dialogues and draw ↑ if the intonation rises and ↓ if it falls.

A: You're going to help that NGO, aren't you?
B: I'm not sure yet. Maybe I am.

A: You're going to help that NGO, aren't you?
B: Of course I am, you know that!

11 Complete the sentences with *rising intonation* or *falling intonation*.

1 When we know the answer to a question and just need confirmation, we use ________.
2 When we are not sure of the answer to a question and we need the other person to give it to us, we use ________.

12 Practice saying the sentences. Pay attention to the intonation.

1 You're going to the park, aren't you? ↑ You love going there!

You're going to the park, aren't you? ↓ Your brother told me.

2 Look at this picture. We were at grandma's house, weren't we? ↑ I don't recognize the background.

Look at this picture. We were at grandma's house, weren't we? ↓ I recognize the background.

Workbook p. 149

WRITING

A Photo-Essay

Before Writing

1 **Plan your photo-essay.**

1. What is it going to be about?
2. What is the purpose of the photo-essay?
3. Who is going to read it?
4. How long will the text be?
5. Where can you get the images for the photo-essay?
6. Are you going to interview the people or use interviews from some other source?

Drafting

2 **Make a draft of your photo-essay.**

3 **Share your photo-essay with a classmate and ask for his/her opinion. Make adjustments, if necessary.**

Final Writing

4 **Make the final version of your photo-essay. Share it on #MAKERS Digital <www.richmondmakers.com> using the hashtag #MyPhotoEssay.**

INVESTIGATE

Photo-essays in my country are usually about ___________.

Collect Data

- Select the sources where you will look for the photo-essays.
- Identify what you consider a photo-essay and save the sources to collect data.
- Follow the published photo-essays for a week.
- Identify the main themes of the photo-essays.
- Take notes on your findings.

Source	Theme of the Photo-Essay

Analyze the Data

- How many different themes could you observe?
- Do the themes vary according to where the photo-essays are published?

Draw a Conclusion

Photo-essays in my country are usually about ___________.

1 **Reflect on your conclusion and discuss.**

1. Was your hypothesis confirmed?
2. Do you think people prefer to read photo-essays than other types of publications? Why?
3. What are the advantages and limitations of photo-essays?

2 **Share your ideas on #MAKERS Digital <www.richmondmakers.com>. Use the hashtag #PhotoEssayAnalysis.**

LOCAL AND GLOBAL

1 **Analyze the ranking. Why do you think these are the most dangerous cities in the world?**

THE 5 MOST DANGEROUS CITIES IN THE WORLD

Rank	City	Country	Homicide Rate (per 100,000)
1	Los Cabos	Mexico	111.33
2	Caracas	Venezuela	111.19
3	Acapulco	Mexico	106.63
4	Natal	Brazil	102.56
5	Tijuana	Mexico	100.77

Based on ‹https://www.worldatlas.com/articles/most-dangerous-cities-in-the-world.html›. Accessed on July 24, 2018.

2 **Research and take notes on your findings.**

1 What factors contribute to a high homicide rate?

2 What is your city or town's homicide rate?

3 **Reflect on your findings.**

1 Considering the ranking in activity 1, would you say that your city or town is dangerous?

2 What can be done to make cities in general safer? What about your city?

IMAGINE

Imagine there were no conflicts.

1 **Research into the concept. Bring your research to be discussed in class.**

RTV

2 **Scan the QR code and read the magazine article. Then discuss the questions with a classmate.**

1 How can conflicts be good for people?

2 Do you agree with the information in the article? Why?

8

CREATIVE MINDS

OBJECTIVES

- Read about and understand ways to boost creativity.
- Use expressions with *do* and *make* to talk about usual activities.
- Listen to someone's opinion about the world forty years from now.
- Give your opinion about changes in the future.
- Read and understand memes.
- Create a meme.
- Talk about innovation.
- Reflect on how to develop creativity.

Read the questions and discuss.

1. Do you consider yourself a creative person?
2. Do you agree that creativity is innate? Or is it something that can be developed?
3. How can people become more creative?
4. Do you think that creative people are more likely to make discoveries and invent new things? Why?

Richmond

#MAKERS
DIGITAL

1

2

3

4

5

6

7

RTV

1. **The images on page 102 show some ways to boost creativity. Read the ideas below and match them to the corresponding images.**
   - a ☐ Devour knowledge.
   - b ☐ Think about something in the future.
   - c ☐ Travel, take a bus or just go for a walk.
   - d ☐ Make a creativity room.
   - e ☐ Try something new.
   - f ☐ Move your eyes to boost creative thinking.
   - g ☐ Do some physical exercise.

2. **Choose an idea from activity 1 to describe the following actions.**
   1. Jane is turning her spare room into an atelier. ______
   2. Kirk visited 15 countries in 3 months. ______
   3. Joe goes running whenever he feels stressed. ______
   4. Saul and Kim are taking circus classes. They want to join the charity group that visits sick kids in hospitals. ______
   5. Denise wants to read fifteen books this year. ______
   6. Candy and Paul are trying to create an NGO that will help kids with hearing disabilities. ______
   7. Mick learned how to make facial expressions with a great video. ______

3. **In your opinion, which of the ways to boost creativity is...**
   - a the most difficult to perform?
   - b the one that demands the most physical preparation?
   - c the one that can also expose you to different cultures?

React!

4. **Read what people do to put their imagination to work and feel more creative. Then leave a comment.**

@Abby_O'Connor I always go for a walk before I start studying for an exam. It helps me clean my mind and start fresh.

@Daniel_Agishev When I have an important meeting, I usually go to the gym the night before and I work out really hard.

@Kellie_Paterson I like to learn new things every day. I try to take a different way home from the office and look for different places in the city to visit. I pay attention to everything that changes around me.

@Bill_Jonathan I love reading. I mean, I don't sit still in a rocking chair if that's what you're thinking! I listen to audio books while I'm biking and when I'm jogging too.

______

______

I Wonder

5. **Write a question about how artists usually get inspiration for their work. Then look for the answer.**

______

______

99 Great! 99 Interact

LANGUAGE 1

1 **Read the expressions from the box and write them in the correct column.**

(one's) hair/nails   a decision
a difference   breakfast/lunch/dinner
friends   money   progress
the cooking   the dishes
the housework   the right thing

 **do** some exercise	 **make** a creativity room

2 **Use some of the expressions from activity 1 to complete the text messages.**

1 Friend

Do you want to go to the party with me?

Oh, yes. I just need to ___________. I want it curly today. It will only take a few minutes.

OK, I'm on my way, then.

2 Friend

My brother is always complaining that he needs to ___________ by himself.

Why don't you help him?

But I do! I cook and ___________ every day!

3 Friend

How are the kids doing at the new school?

They are doing great! They are very smart, so we expect them to ___________ very quickly.

4 Friend

Melissa, are you at home? You have to leave this room! Go out, ___________ some ___________. You're always alone.

Mom, I have friends, OK? We just don't like to hang out at the mall like everybody. We prefer to talk online. Like we are doing right now.

5 Friend

I've just finished my plans for the summer. I'm going to learn Italian.

You're going to study during summer holidays? Lucky you! I have to find a part-time job and ___________.

3 **Write sentences for the images using the words given and the verbs *do* or *make*.**

1 
difference

____

2 
hair

____

3 
dishes

____

4 
decision

____

My Glossary   Study Space

4 **Complete Ruth's testimony below with the words from the box.**

develop   encourage
room   stifle   stimulated

At school, I had a great teacher that really (1) ___________ our creativity. When people (2) ___________ our artistic side, we can develop different skills and be ready for different challenges.
On the other hand, if people (3) ___________ our creativity, we may not be able to (4) ___________ it. Brainstorm sessions would be useless, and we wouldn't have much (5) ___________ for creativity. So the best thing is to keep imagining things and developing our creative mind.

LISTENING AND SPEAKING

1 47 **Bea is being interviewed about her beliefs about the world forty years from now. Check what you think she'll mention. Then listen and confirm your guesses.**

a ☐ education
b ☐ means of communication
c ☐ technology
d ☐ creativity
e ☐ food
f ☐ cell phones
g ☐ teamwork
h ☐ shopping
i ☐ housework
j ☐ relationships

2 48 **Listen again and answer the questions.**

1 According to what Bea mentions at the beginning of the interview, what's not going to change?

____

2 What's one area she believes will change a lot?

____

3 Does she think people will go to schools forty years from now?

____

4 What skills does she mention?

____

5 What is her opinion on creativity?

____

3 **Do you agree with Bea's opinion about creativity? Why?**

4 **Look at the images and retell, in your own words, what Bea had to say about these items.**

1 

____

2 

____

Buzzwords

"I mean, we're still going to [...] ***hit the gym*** *to do some exercise..."*

What does "hit the gym" mean? Look it up!

Pronunciation

5 **Read Bea's statement. How would you pronounce the words "focus" and "development"?**

"People will have to be creative and **focus** on the **development** of new stuff, but it's not going to be easy."

6 49 **Listen again and practice saying the sentence.**

7 **Read the following words. How do you think they are pronounced?**

color country coupon dangerous
develop focus gif meme
status sweet tuition valet

8 50 **Most of the words in activity 7 are commonly mispronounced. Listen and practice saying them.**

Study Space

9 **In pairs, talk about how the words from the box relate to the images below.**

computers environment housing
means of communication pollution
robots technology work

1 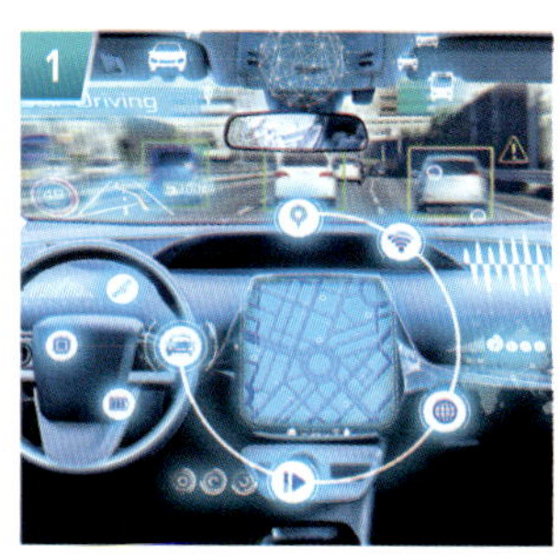

2 

10 **Think about life twenty years from now. Are the images in activity 9 part of this future? If so, how? If not, why? Choose one of the topics you related to them in activity 9 and answer these questions in your notebook.**

11 **Share your ideas with a classmate and ask for his/her opinion. Make adjustments, if necessary.**

12 **Record an audio of your opinion and share it on #MAKERS Digital <www.richmondmakers.com>. Use the hashtag #LifeIn20Years.**

READING

Before Reading

1 Look at the images below and answer the questions.

1 What kind of texts can you see? ______________________________

2 Where can you find these texts? ______________________________

3 What is part of these texts? ______________________________

4 Are they formal or informal? How do you know? ______________________________

5 What do they have in common? ______________________________

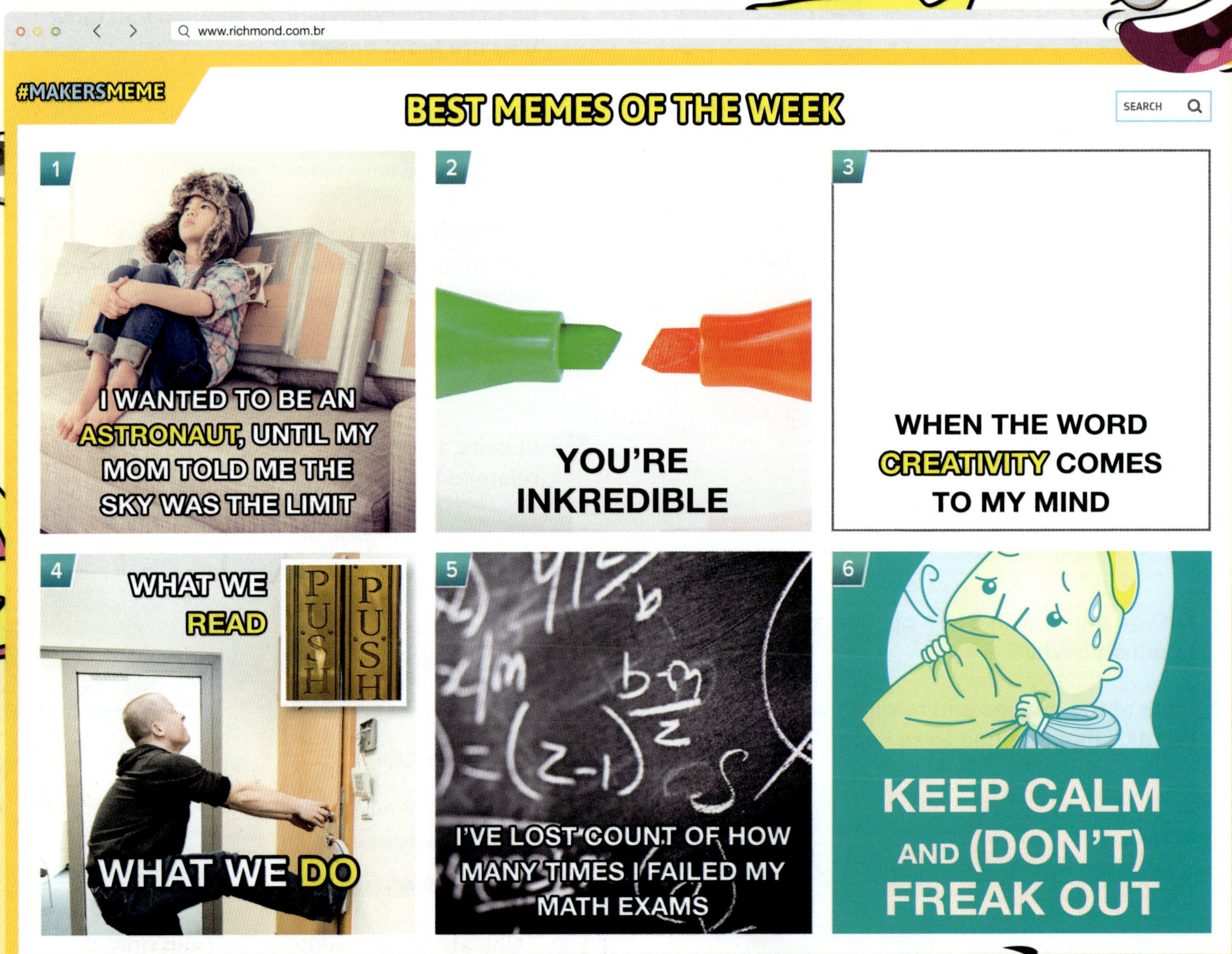

2 Discuss the questions with a classmate.

1 What is a meme?

2 What are memes for?

3 Who usually creates them?

4 Who are the readers of memes?

5 Why do they have such a universal appeal?

6 Is it always easy to understand the fun behind the messages? Why?

Unit 5 Architecture Fair

1 Look at the images and discuss the questions with a classmate.

The Dancing House

Casa Milà

Museum of Tomorrow

Fallingwater

1 Where do you think each of these buildings is located?

2 When do you think they were built?

3 Do you like them? Why?

4 Are you interested in architecture?

2 Do some research and fill in the fact file about the buildings in activity 1.

	The Dancing House	Casa Milà	Museum of Tomorrow	Fallingwater
Where is it located?				
When was it opened?				
How long did it take to be completed?				
Who was the architect in charge?				
What is its style?				

3 Plan a fair of famous buildings in your country. Follow the instructions.

1 Choose some famous buildings in your country and research into them.

2 Reproduce a fact file like the one in activity 2 and complete it with information about the buildings you chose.

3 If possible, visit the buildings and take pictures of them. If not, find images of them.

4 Hold the fair.

1 Present the buildings you selected to visitors.

2 You may ask them to speculate about the buildings before revealing the information you gathered.

3 Ask the visitors which building was their favorite and why.

Glossary

WELCOME

aim at to have a particular purpose

enthusiastic very interested in something or excited by it

forecaster a person who predicts or estimates a future event

insight a clear, deep and usually sudden understanding of a situation

malady a disease

no wonder it is not surprising

profit to gain advantage from something

refurbish to renovate or redecorate a house, apartment or building

replace to take the place of something

revolve around to treat something as the most important element

take over to begin to have control of something

theorize to form a supposition about something

timetabled scheduled to take place at a particular time

treatable able to be cured, especially medically

visionary having original ideas about what the future will or could be like

whammy an event with a powerful and unpleasant impact

workforce the group of people who work in a company, industry, country etc.

UNIT 1

amazing surprising and impressive

audition a short performance that tests if someone's skills are suitable for an event or group

awful very bad or unpleasant

ballroom dancing a type of dancing such as the waltz or tango

bland without strong features or characteristics; uninteresting

blindfolded having the eyes covered by a blindfold

blunt frank and not trying to be polite

captivating very interesting or attractive in a way that takes all someone's attention

cast the actors taking part in a play, film or other production

coach someone who is responsible for training a person or a team

come across to give a certain impression

costume clothes that performers wear in a play, film etc.

dig into to try to find information about something

EDM Electronic Dance Music

failure lack of success

falter to move or speak without confidence or with pauses

in the limelight getting a lot of attention from the public

joy something that makes you feel happy

lyrics the words in a song

mold a container into which you pour a liquid substance so that it hardens in the shape of the container

moving producing strong emotion, especially melancholy

nail to perform something perfectly

pay off to bring benefits

remotely small in degree

scenography the design of theatrical scenery

settle for less to accept something worse than what you deserve

slim small

stress to give emphasis or importance to something

stunning extremely beautiful

tactful careful not to hurt people

tally mark a mark registering an amount or quantity

terrific excellent

tune to adjust a musical instrument to the correct or uniform pitch

willing ready to do something

UNIT 2

assume to accept something as true without question or proof

barefoot wearing nothing on the feet

bring up to take care of a child until he/she becomes mature

chopstick a small stick used as an eating utensil, especially in some Asian cultures

custom a traditional way of behaving or doing something that is particular to a society

cutlery forks, knives and spoons

fairness impartial and just treatment without discrimination or favoritism

freedom the power or right to act, speak or think as one wants

frown upon disapprove of

jaywalk to cross a street at a place where you are not allowed to do it

kindness the quality of being friendly, generous and considerate

loyalty a strong feeling of support

minced cut up into small pieces

open-mindedness the ability to take new ideas into consideration

overcome to succeed in dealing with a problem or difficulty

peculiarity a strange or unusual feature or habit

perseverance persistence in doing something difficult

readiness the state of being prepared for something

regardless of not affected or influenced by something

reliability the quality of being able to be trusted

selfishness lack of consideration for other people

straightforward honest and frank

sympathy a feeling of understanding for someone who is suffering

trustworthy able to be trusted

usefulness the quality of having utility

UNIT 3

boundary the edge or limit of something

camp a place with temporary accommodation, typically used by soldiers or refugees

coexist to exist in harmony

compulsory necessary by law or a rule

concern to be relevant to someone; to affect or involve someone

current happening now

dare to have the courage to do something

daydream to spend time thinking about something pleasant, especially when you should be focusing on something else

dismantle to end a political or economic system; to get rid of an institution

eloquent giving a clear, strong message

imply to suggest as a logical consequence

infer to conclude from evidence rather than from explicit statements

issue an important topic or problem for debate

march an event in which many people walk through a public place to express their position concerning a public issue

purge to remove a group of people considered undesirable from a place in a violent way

renowned known by many people; famous

segregation the policy of keeping people from different groups—especially different races—separate

speech a formal discourse delivered to an audience

stand out be easily noticeable

willingly happily and enthusiastically

UNIT 4

assess to make a judgment about a situation

cognitive involving conscious intellectual activity

convey to communicate

distress extreme anxiety, unhappiness or pain

enhance to intensify, to increase

figure a number, especially one which is part of official statistics

genuine authentic

journal a daily record of events of a personal nature; a diary

mild not severe or serious

relieve to make pain or distress less severe or serious

self-esteem confidence in one's own worth or abilities

unwind to relax after a period of tension

UNIT 5

advertise to draw attention to a product, service or event in a public medium in order to promote it

assignment a task given to someone as part of a course

blinding remarkably skillful and enjoyable

complement to add to something in order to improve it

consent permission for something to happen

cubist in the style of the early 20th-century artistic movement in which perspective with a single viewpoint was abandoned

deliberate done intentionally

display to put something in a prominent place to make it easily seen

drawing a picture made with a pencil, pen or crayon, rather than paint

due planned for a certain date and time

exhibition a public display of works of art

flattering pleasing or gratifying

fond finding something enjoyable or pleasant

frightening making someone afraid; terrifying

hypothetical based on ideas or situations that are possible, rather than real

impressive evoking admiration

own to have, to possess

portrait a painting, drawing, photograph or engraving of a person

portray to depict someone in a work of art or in literature

pottery the craft of making objects from clay

sketch a rough or unfinished drawing, often made as a first undetailed draft of a more finished product

stick to to continue doing or using something

thriller a novel, play or movie with an exciting plot, typically involving crime or espionage

versatile able to adapt to different purposes or activities

wax a substance made from beeswax used to make candles and models

UNIT 6

appliance a piece of equipment designed to perform a specific task

brand product(s) with a particular name produced by a particular company

chore a routine task, especially a household one

consumerism the belief that it is good for a society or person to buy a lot of goods and services

customer a person or company that buys products or services

cut down on to reduce the size or amount of something

deadline a specific moment by which something must be done

defrost to become or make something warmer so that it is no longer frozen

delay to happen later than was planned or expected

device a piece of mechanical or electronic equipment

gadget a small mechanical or electronic device, especially one that does something useful

lawn an area with grass in the garden/yard of a house or park

lightweight made of thin material or weighing less than usual

logo a symbol or design used by an organization to identify itself or its products

manage to deal successfully with something or with a particular situation

mow to cut down grass with a machine

reminder something that causes someone to remember a task or an event

slogan a short or memorable phrase used in publicity

unsuitable not right or inappropriate for a particular person or situation

worn out used so much that it has become damaged or no longer fit for use

wrinkled having lines or folds, especially fabric

UNIT 7

apology a statement to tell someone that you are sorry for something

argue to speak to someone in an angry way because you disagree with him/her

belongings a person's possessions that can be moved

commitment an agreement to do something in the future

course direction

flee to run away from a place or situation of danger

forlorn abandoned; not cared for and with nobody in it

greed intense desire for something, especially money or power

handle to deal with

mediate to intervene in a dispute in order to bring about a reconciliation or to find a solution

misunderstanding failure to understand something correctly

prevent to keep something from happening

prom a formal dance at school, especially held at the end of the academic year to celebrate graduation

resolve to find a solution to something

smuggler a person who moves things illegally into a certain place or out of it

spread an increase in the amount of something or its growth or development

UNIT 8

appeal the quality of being attractive or interesting

atelier a workshop or studio used by an artist or designer

boost to increase something or make it better

brief concise; using few words

devour to look at something or read it enthusiastically and with interest

enroll to officially register as a student in a course

freak out to behave in a wild and irrational way because of extreme emotions

inhibit to prevent something from happening or to make it less frequent

innate inborn; natural

NGO a nonprofit organization that operates independently of any government

refrain to stop oneself from doing something

remodel to change the structure or form of something, especially a building or part of it

stifle to prevent an activity or idea

stimulate to encourage

Infinitive	Past Simple	Past Participle
be	was/were	been
become	became	become
break	broke	broken
build	built	built
buy	bought	bought
choose	chose	chosen
come	came	come
cut	cut	cut
deal	dealt	dealt
do	did	done
draw	drew	drawn
drive	drove	driven
eat	ate	eaten
fall	fell	fallen
feel	felt	felt
fight	fought	fought
find	found	found
flee	fled	fled
fly	flew	flown
foresee	foresaw	foreseen
get	got	got/gotten
give	gave	given
go	went	gone
grow	grew	grown
have	had	had
hear	heard	heard
hit	hit	hit
hold	held	held
hurt	hurt	hurt
keep	kept	kept
know	knew	known
leave	left	left
lend	lent	lent

Infinitive	Past Simple	Past Participle
lose	lost	lost
make	made	made
mean	meant	meant
meet	met	met
pay	paid	paid
put	put	put
read	read	read
ride	rode	ridden
run	ran	run
say	said	said
see	saw	seen
sell	sold	sold
send	sent	sent
set	set	set
shine	shone	shone
shut	shut	shut
sing	sang	sung
sit	sat	sat
sleep	slept	slept
speak	spoke	spoken
spend	spent	spent
stand	stood	stood
take	took	taken
teach	taught	taught
tell	told	told
think	thought	thought
throw	threw	thrown
understand	understood	understood
wake	woke	woken
wear	wore	worn
win	won	won
write	wrote	written

Name: Class:

1 Scan the letter to the editor and check the sentence that best summarizes the reader's opinion.

1 ☐ It's never too late to make your dreams come true, so take acting lessons.

2 ☐ Acting lessons can help you develop social and professional skills.

3 ☐ It's time to invest in yourself and become a professional actor.

The importance of acting lessons

By Joshua Tribiani, Brooklyn, NY

I'm writing in response to the article "The importance of acting lessons" that was published in the last issue. Although the article focuses on the importance of such lessons for professionals or potential actors and actresses, it is important to mention that acting lessons can benefit everybody who takes them. Actually, if you have another professional aspiration and want to improve a set of important social and professional skills, acting lessons can be of great help. Here are at least two skills that can be developed through them. The first one is confidence. When acting, actors have to go through different situations in which they will find themselves under pressure, be it on stage or on a set in front of several cameras. It can also help shy people build a stronger sense of confidence and feel more comfortable in their own skin.

The second is public speaking. It is an important skill that many professionals lack nowadays. The ability to speak clearly and articulately is fundamental when acting. So, people who feel very nervous in front of an audience may get some helpful tips on how to succeed in this kind of situation.

In brief, there is still a misconception about who should take acting classes, and we must be very careful not to reinforce such ideas. Besides, many people miss great opportunities for self-development because of lack of information. Acting can help us get better at many different skills besides the ones that I have mentioned. I just hope more people will start taking acting lessons even if they don't intend to pursue an acting career.

2 Read the letter to the editor in activity 1. Then answer the questions below and underline evidence of the answers in the letter.

1 Why don't many people take acting classes?

____

2 Why can acting help people feel more confident?

____

3 How can acting help people with public speaking?

____

3 Correct the sentences below according to the text in activity 1.

1 Acting lessons can benefit everyone. However, people who have professional aspirations other than acting shouldn't take them.

____

____

2 When people improve their public-speaking skills, they feel more comfortable in their own skin.

____

____

3 There are no misconceptions related to who can benefit from acting classes, so we don't need to be careful about this topic.

____

____

4 The article "The importance of acting lessons" focuses on the importance of acting lessons for everybody.

____

____

4 Complete the sentences below based on Joshua's letter and on your opinions.

1 I agree with Joshua's opinion. However, ______________________________

______________________________.

2 People can improve their self-esteem and public-speaking skills when taking acting lessons. On the other hand, they ______________________________

______________________________.

3 Besides the topics mentioned, ______________________________

______________________________.

5 **Use linking words and the prompts in parentheses to complete the sentences.**

1 Flamenco is a solo dance characterized by hand clapping, percussive footwork and body movements. ______________ (addition), it is usually accompanied by a singer and a guitar player.

2 ______________ (contrast) many people think the haka is used to intimidate opponents, it is also used when groups come together in peace.

3 Italian folk dancing is much varied. Each town has its specific dance. ______________ (summarizing), if you want to know more about all of them, it's going to take a long time!

4 A kabuki performance often only shows part of an entire story. ______________ (conclusion), it would be good to read a little about the story a performance is about before going to the show.

6 **Match the sentences in activity 5 to the images below. Then use words from the box to express your opinion about them.**

amazing awful captivating
fabulous fantastic hilarious
horrible stunning terrible terrific

a 

____

____

b 

____

____

c 

____

____

d 

____

____

7 **Which ungradable adjectives did you choose to write sentences in activity 6? List them below and write the corresponding gradable adjective next to each of them.**

1 ______________________________

2 ______________________________

3 ______________________________

4 ______________________________

8 **Use the linking words from the box to take part in the dialogues. You can repeat them once.**

besides that however
in summary on the contrary so

1
Marco: Why don't you want to go to the flamenco festival with me?
You: ______________________________

2
Jade: I was thinking about watching a kabuki performance next Friday. What do you think?
You: ______________________________

3
Tyler: Maybe we could take Italian folk classes together! I'd love it!
You: ______________________________

4
Anne: I've always wanted to be a flamenco dancer, but my parents think it is a waste of time!
You: ______________________________

9 **Use the ungradable adjectives from activity 6 and the intensifiers below to write true sentences about yourself.**

absolutely completely
exceptionally particularly totally

1 best movie: ______________________________

2 favorite band/singer: ______________________________

3 worst vacation: ______________________________

4 saddest book: ______________________________

5 funniest meme: ______________________________

Extension

Name: Class:

1 What type of text is this? Check the correct option.

a [ ] A news report.
b [ ] An online magazine article.
c [ ] A post on a social network.

100%

Avoiding Cross-Cultural Faux Pas in RUSSIA

Russia is considered an innovative country in many ways. However, it's also a country full of traditions and superstitions. Because most of these may be unknown to foreigners, they can cause some confusion. Here are some dos and don'ts in Russia:

NO SHOES

When you visit someone's home in Russia, it's expected that you immediately take off your shoes. Streets in the country tend to be very dirty, so people avoid carrying the dirt into their homes. Your host will probably offer you slippers to wear inside the house.

FLOWERS MAY BE RUDE

We tend to think of flowers as a romantic gift. In Russia, flowers can be a romantic gift too, but it's important to consider some details. First, the number of flowers you give should not be even, unless you are going to a funeral. Second, avoid giving yellow flowers, since they are also considered proper for funerals.

GIFTS ARE WELCOME

Hosts are very concerned with your visit to their home in Russia. They've probably spent money to keep you comfortable and prepared a delicious meal. So, it's polite to bring a gift with you when visiting someone in Russia. You don't have to bring a gift for everybody in the house, only for the hosts. Chocolate and flowers (see our tips about flowers) are much appreciated.

NO MONEY EXCHANGE AT NIGHT

Let's imagine you owe someone some money. You should pay it back, right? In Russia, you have to pay it back too! Just make sure you don't do it after nightfall. Many Russians believe it's a bad omen.

Based on <https://www.goabroad.com/articles/study-abroad/10-ways-not-to-offend-people-in-russia>. Accessed on July 31, 2018.

2 Read the article about Russia from a travelers' online magazine and check the topics mentioned.

1 [ ] The cleanliness of Russian streets.
2 [ ] When (not) to wear shoes.
3 [ ] Table manners.
4 [ ] What to wear in sacred places.
5 [ ] Gift-giving.
6 [ ] Greeting people.
7 [ ] Habits related to money.

3 Read the online magazine article again and answer the questions.

1 Why should we take off our shoes when we visit someone in Russia?

______

______

2 What should we pay attention to when we give flowers in Russia?

______

______

3 Why should we bring a gift when we visit someone in Russia?

______

______

4 Why shouldn't we exchange money at night?

______

______

4 Check the best meaning for the word "omen".

1 [ ] A sign that you did something embarrassing.
2 [ ] A sign that something will happen.
3 [ ] A sign that you don't trust the other person.

5 Is anything considered a bad omen in your country?

______

______

6 Based on the information from the online magazine article, do you think it would be difficult for you to adapt to the Russian culture? Why?

______

______

7 Complete the chart.

Adjective	Noun
Committed	
Compassionate	
	Courage
Fair	
	Honesty
Kind	
	Loyalty
Motivated	
Reliable	
	Respect

8 Complete the sentences using nouns from activity 7.

1 I think nurses need a good dose of ______ because they help people who are going through a difficult time.

2 It's beautiful to see ______ among friends. They're really there for each other in all moments of life.

3 When you feel true ______, nothing can stop you.

4 Judges need to consider all arguments carefully to make a coherent decision. There is no justice without ______.

5 In my country, we must always show ______ when we are in the presence of teachers. We need to be polite and considerate.

6 One of the most important values in my family is ______. We try never to be afraid of challenges.

9 Choose people who, in your opinion, represent the values in activity 8 and explain why. You can think of your family, friends or even famous people.

1 To me, ______ represents ______ because ______.

2 To me, ______ represents ______ because ______.

3 To me, ______ represents ______ because ______.

4 To me, ______ represents ______ because ______.

5 To me, ______ represents ______ because ______.

6 To me, ______ represents ______ because ______.

10 Check the right sentences. Then rewrite the wrong ones, correcting them.

1 We don't can be late or we'll miss our flight.

______

2 He can speak five languages, so he'll be the perfect companion for this trip.

______

3 You should to pack your bags, we're leaving tomorrow morning.

______

4 You mustn't not forget your sunscreen. The next two days will be very sunny.

______

5 We to have buy groceries for the weekend before we leave.

______

6 Remember you shouldn't wear shoes in Grandma's house.

______

11 Complete each sentence with the correct modal verb, according to the meanings in parentheses.

1 You ______ help your family with house chores. (obligation)

2 You ______ do your homework right after school. (suggestion)

3 You ______ walk barefoot in your home. (permission)

4 You ______ disrespect people. (prohibition)

5 You ______ go on an exchange to learn a new language. (possibility)

12 Check the sentence that has a similar meaning to the first one.

1 You are authorized to take your dog on the plane.

a ☐ You can take your dog on the plane.

b ☐ You should take your dog on the plane.

2 You are forbidden to take pictures of this exhibition.

a ☐ You don't have to take pictures of this exhibition.

b ☐ You mustn't take pictures of this exhibition.

3 You are obliged to pass your tests if you want to graduate.

a ☐ You can pass your tests if you want to graduate.

b ☐ You must pass your tests if you want to graduate.

Extension

Name: Class:

1 Complete the opinion article with the expressions from the box.

As far as I'm concerned I'm sure
I dare say I share their views
In my opinion It goes without saying
It seems to me that

New Immigration Policy in the U.S. Is Too Extreme

Most people all over the world are shocked by Donald Trump's new policy of separating families at the U.S. borders, and (1) ________________, but many of them are wondering how the entire administration obeys the orders of literally taking children from their mothers' arms. (2) ________________, the objective is to make it crystal clear that illegal immigration will not be tolerated, no matter what it takes. (3) ________________ this administration thinks that extreme measures like this are the best tool to prevent people from coming illegally to the country, but is that really the answer?

This month, attorney general Jeff Sessions announced that any person who arrives illegally in the country will face criminal charges and, because children can't be in jail like adults, that means that families will be separated–the adults going to a jail-like facility and the children being held in shelters or foster care. The result of this policy is the heartbreaking scenes of terrified parents and children at the borders.

(4) ________________, this policy is too extreme, since before this administration families of illegal immigrants would be kept together in government facilities until they returned to their countries.

This is not the first harsh policy of Trump's administration– (5) ________________ you will remember the president's proposition of building a wall separating the United States from Mexico and his ban on every Muslim entering the country in 2017–and (6) ________________ it won't be the last one. (7) ________________ that fear works to send a message to those considering immigrating to this country. That is the point of these policies.

Adapted from <https://www.smh.com.au/world/north-america/donald-trump-s-immigration-policies-are-cruel-that-s-the-whole-point-20180529-p4zi27.html>. Accessed on July 23, 2018.

2 Read the opinion article again and answer the questions.

1 According to the text, what is the new immigration policy in the U.S. doing?

____

2 According to the author, what is the objective of this new policy?

____

3 Who made the announcement of the new immigration policy?

____

4 What will happen to adults who cross the borders illegally?

____

5 What will happen to the children?

____

6 According to the author, what is the result of these new policies?

____

7 What happened to families of illegal immigrants in the previous administration?

____

3 Read the article again and check the correct options. More than one answer may be possible.

1 The text contains...
- a ☐ facts.
- b ☐ opinions.
- c ☐ a personal story.

2 The facts are presented...
- a ☐ as an opinion.
- b ☐ with sources.
- c ☐ mentioning official spokespeople.

3 The author...
- a ☐ is shocked by the new policy.
- b ☐ thinks that extreme immigration policies work better.
- c ☐ doesn't think this policy is the best way to handle illegal immigration.

4 What other harsh policies are mentioned?
- a ☐ Banning immigrants based on their religious beliefs.
- b ☐ Building a wall separating the U.S. from Mexico.
- c ☐ Expelling all illegal immigrants.

4 Write sentences agreeing or disagreeing with the opinions below.

1 People tend to think that being a refugee is a choice.

____

2 Very little has been done to prevent the wars that force people to emigrate.

____

3 Ensuring that no one fleeing from wars finds closed borders should be a priority for every country.

____

4 If there were no wars, starvation or political prosecutions, there would be no refugees in the world.

____

5 Complete the sentences with the words from the box, the verb to be and *may*, *might* or *could*.

closed fit good tired worried

1 Sasha has been studying since 7 a.m. It's 5 p.m. now. She ______________.

2 Steven's soccer team is losing the match. He ______________.

3 It's 10 p.m. The coffee shop ______________.

4 Matt runs 10 km every day. He ______________.

5 Many people are ordering the new sandwich. It ______________.

6 Rewrite the sentences below using *may*, *might* or *could*.

1 I think Tom wants to go to the party.

____

2 It's possible that you'll see John downtown because he also works there.

____

3 It's possible that I will study in Japan when I grow up.

____

4 Going to the conference tomorrow is a possibility for me.

____

5 I think they have the flu.

____

6 Extreme rain possibly causes floods.

____

7 Read the dialogues and circle the correct replies. More than one option may be possible.

1 **A:** I support the rights of refugees.
B: **Me too. / Me neither. / I do too.**

2 **A:** I don't like the idea of immigrants being deported.
B: **Me too. / I don't like it either. / Me neither.**

3 **A:** I think women are equal to men.
B: **I do too. / I don't either. / Me too.**

4 **A:** I believe every country should receive and help refugees.
B: **Me neither. / Me too. / I don't believe it either.**

5 **A:** I don't agree with his point of view.
B: **I do too. / Me too. / Me neither.**

8 Read the pairs of sentences and write S if they mean the same or D if they have different meanings.

1 There's a possibility that this person in the picture is my cousin Jane.
This person in the picture could be my cousin Jane. ___

2 These shoes look expensive.
These shoes couldn't be expensive. ___

3 This might be our bus.
It's possible that this is our bus. ___

4 I'm not certain that this is my pencil case.
This may not be my pencil case. ___

5 This may not be the best idea to solve this problem.
This is probably a good idea to solve this problem. ___

9 Cross out the mistakes in the sentences below and correct them.

1 **A:** I think plastic surgery should be forbidden for people under 18.
B: I too. ______________

2 Are you taking an umbrella? It couldn't rain. ______________

3 I think you might not like this book. Do you want to borrow it? ______________

4 **A:** I don't think people should gossip.
B: I think so too. ______________

5 **A:** I don't like selfish people.
B: Me too. ______________

Extension

 Name: Class:

1 Read Megan's blog post. Then answer the questions.

www.richmond.com.br

Nowadays it is very difficult to find someone who has an organized routine. Having time for yourself is rare when you live in a big cosmopolitan city. Until some time ago, I thought that it wasn't necessary, I didn't need some me time because all I had to do was work and study. People used to tell me that I was always stressed out, that I had an angry face and so on. Two months ago, I ran into an old friend of mine and we talked a little bit about how our lives had changed and she told me that she was a yoga teacher. She explained some of the possible consequences of stress, as well as the benefits of yoga, and I was shocked! Now I know the importance of having time to unwind or do the things you want, not only your obligations. If you have the same routine as I used to have and can't find a way out, try some yoga lessons, take some time off, go for a walk... There are so many options out there! We just have to be bold and try them out until we find the ones we like best.

1 What's Megan's opinion about the importance of relaxation?

______

2 Why didn't Megan worry about making time for herself?

______

3 How did Megan use to come across to other people?

______

4 What made Megan change her routine and find some time for herself?

______

5 What does she recommend to people who would like to change their routines?

______

2 Read Megan's blog post again and find synonyms to replace the words highlighted in these sentences.

1 Now I know it's important to **relax**. ______
2 I was always **really tense**. ______
3 If you can't find **your own space**, try something new. ______
4 Now I have **time for myself**. ______
5 It's important to be **brave** and try new things. ______

3 Use the synonyms you wrote in activity 2 to make sentences about the importance of taking some time off for yourself.

1 ______
2 ______
3 ______
4 ______
5 ______

4 Complete Julia's comment on Megan's blog post with the words from the box in the correct form (adjective, noun or verb).

laugh meditate relax

www.richmond.com.br

>> Comments

1 **Julia** says: August 30, 2018 at 10:50 A.M.

I agree with you, Megan. In our hectic routines, it's hard to find some time to (1) ______. However, more and more, specialists recommend we make time, even if it means just 5 minutes per day. As you said, strategies for (2) ______ might vary from (3) ______ to laughing with friends. It seems simple, but a lot of people have a hard time interrupting their activities to (4) ______. We should also keep up with positivity and find reasons to (5) ______ with people around us. That's what I try to do! So, remember that (6) ______ is among the top five activities that help us relax and feel re-energized. Keep calm and laugh!

5 Read the counselor's advice and circle the correct options to complete it.

"People usually do physical exercise because it helps their bodies to stay strong, but what about mental health? Many people don't give the appropriate importance to mental health and if you don't either, you (1) **might like** / **are liking** / **liked** to know more about its benefits. Taking care of mental health is extremely important because when we (2) **will be** / **might be** / **are** mentally healthy, we (3) **enjoys** / **enjoy** / **enjoyed** our life and the people around us. You might miss opportunities to learn and try new things, take risks and even be more creative (4) **unless** / **if** / **when** you care about your mental health. When you realize how important it is, you (5) **will be** / **are** / **be** better able to deal with difficult times and enjoy your life to the fullest."

6 Complete the sentences below with what happens in these situations.

1 If you do physical exercises frequently, __________.

2 When you are too stressed out, __________.

3 __________ unless you stop thinking about your obligations.

4 If you talk about your feelings more often, __________.

5 If you take short breaks while studying, __________.

7 Complete the conversations below with *unless*, *if*, *when* or *provided that*.

1 **Noah:** Now that I study at this new school, I feel that I don't have any friends.

Jane: Maybe ________ you socialize with your classmates, you might feel better.

2 **Chris:** I have many things to do, I'm feeling really stressed out...

Jill: You might continue feeling like this ________ you change your study routine.

3 **Kathy:** I had to walk to school this morning and now I can't feel my legs! Can you believe that?

Mike: I'm sure ________ you start exercising regularly, your body will feel stronger.

4 **Paula:** I don't know why people don't talk to me! What do you think?

Karl: You look too serious! ________ you smile more, people will think you don't like them.

5 **Richard:** I feel worn out... I feel terrible... All I want to do is to sleep. What should I do?

Thomas: You will feel better ________ you take some action and look after yourself a little bit.

8 Now it is your turn to give advice about the situations below. Remember to use conditional sentences.

1 **Paula:** Sometimes I feel so anxious that I can't sleep.

You: __________

2 **Karl:** I don't know how to express my feelings. I find it hard to talk about them.

You: __________

3 **Robert:** My friends say I'm too serious.

You: __________

4 **Ted:** I don't like exercising. What else can I do to stay active?

You: __________

5 **Kelly:** I don't feel comfortable when things change too much.

You: __________

9 Order the words below to make questions.

1 you / Do / get / enough sleep / usually / ?

____

2 activities / do / practice / you / How often / physical / ?

____

3 relieve / you / do / What / stress / to / anxiety / do / and / deal with / ?

____

4 routine / change / Would / your / like to / you / ?

____

5 you / How / do / show / gratitude / for the things / in your life / you / have / ?

____

6 changes / What / believe / do / you / you / make to your routine / starting tomorrow / can / ?

____

10 Answer the questions from activity 9.

1 __________

2 __________

3 __________

4 __________

5 __________

6 __________

Extension

Name: Class:

1 Read the article below. What is the author's opinion about graffiti?

____

www.richmond.com.br

IS GRAFFITI REALLY ART?

What is visual art? According to the Encyclopaedia Britannica, visual art is "a visual object or experience consciously created through an expression of skill or imagination". Although graffiti has been among us since prehistoric times, the big debate over whether it is art or vandalism is much more recent.

Many people claim that it is a form of street art involving complex drawings that represent the artist's, and sometimes the community's, emotions. On the other hand, a significant number of people say it is an action involving deliberate destruction of or damage to public and private property.

To my mind, there are many ways in which you can express your art, and graffiti is one of them. Provided that the artists have the property owners' consent, their walls can serve as big pieces of paper, waiting for artists to beautify them and thus be remembered for their talent. If their art is beautiful or not will depend exclusively on your point of view.

CLOSE

Based on <https://www.graffiti.ee/graffiti-vandalism-art/>. Accessed on July 27, 2018.

2 Complete the statements based on the article.

1 Graffiti has been among us since ______________.

2 The debate over graffiti is ______________.

3 For some people, graffiti drawings represent not only the emotions of the artist, but also the ones of ______________.

4 For other people, graffiti ______________.

3 Find an example of collocation in the text. Look for an adjective + a preposition.

____

4 Complete the collocations in the sentences with a preposition from the box.

about	at	for (3x)	of

1 I'm not fond ______ comedy movies. I'd rather watch an action one!

2 Zaha Hadid is known ______ her excellent architectural projects, such as the Antwerp Port House in Belgium.

3 Robert Capa is an incredible photographer! He is famous ______ his wartime photographs.

4 I couldn't be more excited ______ my next trip! I'm going to visit many museums and see famous paintings.

5 Michelangelo is still remembered ______ his outstanding sculptures, such as *Madonna of the Stairs* and *Battle of the Centaurs*.

6 Caledonia Curry, or SWOON, is incredibly good ______ using her graffiti art to help rebuild devastated communities.

5 Read the text messages and underline five sentences where *if* is missing. Then rewrite them in your notebook including it.

Marcy: Hey! Take a look at my Art project!

Tom: WOW! That's impressive!!!!!

Marcy: It's gr8, isn't it?! I'm so proud of it! My teacher likes it, he can include it in the end-of-the year exhibition.

Tom: Really??? That'd be awesome! I'm sure he'll select your painting. I mean, look at it! But do you still have Art classes? Mine ended in primary school.

Marcy: We have Art classes every year. I luv it!!!!

Tom: Maybe I had Art classes, I'd be better at drawing. It must be so cool to make your imagination come true.

Marcy: I can teach you some things to you you want.

Tom: I had more time, I'd love to, but…

Marcy: Just let me know you change your mind.

6 Make sentences using the prompts given. There are two possibilities for each item.

1 I would know more about architecture / if / I read more about it

I would know more about architecture if I read more about it.

If I read more about it, I would know more about architecture.

2 if / we won the lottery / we wouldn't buy a new painting

____

____

3 if / I were a dedicated student / I wouldn't go to the movies with my friends so often

____

____

4 I would buy a new camera / if / I had enough money

____

____

5 I would try to learn pottery / if / I didn't have a busy routine

____

____

7 Rewrite the sentences from activity 6 so that they are true for you.

1 _______________

2 _______________

3 _______________

4 _______________

5 _______________

8 Complete Jessica and Marcela's conversation using the correct form of the verbs in parentheses and *would* if necessary.

Jessica: What _________ you _________ (do) if you _________ (be) at home without an internet access?

Marcela: I _________ (try) to find something to watch on cable TV.

Jessica: And if the cable _________ (be) working?

Marcela: I _________ (look) for my parents' old DVDs.

Jessica: And if you _________ (find) them?

Marcela: I _________ (read) a book. _________ you _________ (have) something else to do if you _________ (have) to stay home without the internet?

Jessica: I _________ probably _________ (draw) .

9 Check the best option to complete the sentences.

1 We would see Donatello's famous sculptures...

a ☐ if we were in Italy.

b ☐ if we are in Europe.

c ☐ when we are Italy.

2 If we had the money,...

a ☐ we bought these amazing photographs.

b ☐ we'll buy these amazing photographs.

c ☐ we'd buy these amazing photographs.

3 He would be welcome to join our graffiti team...

a ☐ if he would know our techniques.

b ☐ if he know the techniques.

c ☐ if he knew the techniques.

4 This movie would be very famous...

a ☐ if it is advertised more on TV.

b ☐ if it would be advertised more on TV.

c ☐ if it were advertised more on TV.

10 Look at the images and complete the sentences with the verbs in parentheses and *would* if necessary.

1

If schools _____________ (encourage) the production of Art projects, maybe more students _____________ (discover) their talents.

2

If I _____________ (know) how to express my ideas visually, I _____________ (study) Architecture.

Extension

Name: Class:

1 Read the ads and answer the questions.

a What products are being advertised?

____

b What is the name of the company that is advertisings the product?

____

2 Read the ads again and number the characteristics according to the ad they correspond to.

a ☐ abbreviated brand name
b ☐ brand slogan
c ☐ comparison with other models
d ☐ detailed product functions
e ☐ focus on a special feature
f ☐ long product name
g ☐ targeted at adults in general
h ☐ targeted at housewives

3 Write T (true) or F (false) according to the ads.

1 ☐ Both ads use formal language and give a lot of information.
2 ☐ The way to contact the company has changed.
3 ☐ The name of the company has changed.
4 ☐ The company has produced washing machines for a long time.
5 ☐ The company used to advertise mainly to women.

4 Why do you think the target audience for washing machine ads has changed from "only housewives" to "adults in general"?

____

____

____

5 Write a chore you can do with each device below.

1

2

3

4

5

6

6 Use the verbs and the prompts in the boxes to write about Agatha's life.

~~be~~ have
learn live
write visit

four children and six grandchildren
in many different places
~~married twice~~ nine countries
three languages two books

1 Agatha has been married twice.
2 ______
3 ______
4 ______
5 ______
6 ______

7 Have your grandparents had many experiences like Agatha's? Write four sentences about what they have and haven't done in their lives.

______
______
______
______

8 Circle the correct option to complete each sentence.

1 Mrs. Moore has worked here for **2015** / **twenty-five years**.
2 Jessica has had a dog for **a few weeks now** / **she was 10**.
3 We've been married since **1981** / **five months**.
4 They've known each other for **January** / **over 50 years**.
5 My family and I have lived here since **2006** / **a long time**.
6 Joe has been on the team since **he was 17** / **three years**.

9 Look at the images and write questions and answers about the Thompsons' chores using the present perfect and *yet* or *already*.

The Thompsons

1 Mrs. Thompson – do the dishes

A: Has Mrs. Thompson done the dishes?
B: No, she hasn't. She hasn't done the dishes yet.

2 they – iron the clothes

A: ______
B: ______

3 Jasmine – mow the lawn

A: ______
B: ______

4 they – vacuum the floor

A: ______
B: ______

5 Jonas – do the laundry

A: ______
B: ______

6 Mr. Thompson – make lunch

A: ______
B: ______

Extension

Name: Class:

1 **Look at the text and complete the sentence.**

This type of text is a __________.

www.richmond.com.br

In addition to conflicts between groups of people and internal conflicts, there are people versus nature conflicts. Humanity has always struggled with natural adversity, such as wilderness, storms, hurricanes, volcanoes etc. However, our environment has also been victim of all sorts of attacks. Take a look at two big natural disasters caused by man.

Darvaza Gas Crater, Turkmenistan

In 1971, Soviet geologists thought that Darvaza could be an oil field site. They made a drilling rig and it exposed a large methane gas reservoir. Fearing the environmental impact because of the substantial methane gas release, geologists decided to burn it off. The gas has been burning since then.

Former Aral Sea, Kazakhstan/Uzbekistan

The Aral Sea used to cover an area of 68,000 square kilometers, but due to Soviet irrigation projects, it started shrinking in the 1960s. In 2004, it covered only a surface area of about 17,160 square kilometers. This phenomenon has been called one of the planet's worst environmental disasters. The region's once significant fishing industry has almost disappeared, causing severe unemployment.

Based on <https://www.storyboardthat.com/articles/e/types-of-literary-conflict>; <https://list25.com/25-biggest-man-made-environmental-disasters-in-history/2/>; <https://www.worldatlas.com/articles/the-shrinking-of-the-aral-sea.html>. Accessed on July 25, 2018.

2 **Find the mistakes and correct the sentences according to the photo-essay.**

1 Soviet geologists believed that Darvaza could have methane gas.

____

2 The geologists decided to drain the gas to minimize the environmental impact.

____

3 In 2004, the Aral Sea covered a surface area of about half of its original size.

____

4 The shrinking of the Aral Sea caused full employment.

____

3 **Imagine these images are part of a photo-essay about cities after conflicts. Match them to their captions.**

1

2

( ) The A-bomb Dome is one of the remains of a Hiroshima that few residents recall. The city is now just like any other Japanese city—lots of offices and apartment blocks, nightlife, convenience stores and coffee shops.

Based on <https://www.theguardian.com/cities/2016/apr/18/story-of-cities-hiroshima-japan-nuclear-destruction>. Accessed on July 21, 2018.

( ) The *Berlin* sculpture was unveiled in 1987 and symbolizes the divided city. It is located in a busy commercial area in front of the Kaiser-Wilhelm memorial church, which was badly damaged during WWII.

Based on <https://issuu.com/lefkos/docs/berlin_-_city_as_memory_landscape>. Accessed on July 25, 2018.

4 Complete the sentences with the verbs from the box in the simple past or present perfect.

argue communicate
consider prevent resolve

1 The chancellor __________ with other authorities over immigration laws since she was elected.

2 Yesterday, Ben and Jane __________ to us that they were leaving the country. The conflicts in their region are getting worse and they want a safe place to raise their kids.

3 __________ you __________ the conflict with your brother? It's high time you two got along well!

4 In the past, the government __________ the spread of the disease by distributing masks. They stopped when the situation was under control.

5 __________ you __________ going back to your family's home? After so many years away, maybe you should spend some time with them.

5 Circle the best options to complete the sentences.

1 I **haven't played** / **didn't play** soccer in several months. The gangs are now all over the place and it's not safe to go to the field.

2 My sister **has born** / **was born** in a small town in Syria.

3 We **have lived** / **lived** in the suburbs for five months, but now we're back downtown.

4 Linda **has been** / **went** to Afghanistan three times.

5 My brother **has visited** / **visited** his girlfriend's NGO last month.

6 Write questions for the prompts. Use the correct verb tense and *you*. Follow the example.

1 ever / be / the United States
Have you ever been to the United States?

2 ever / eat / Thai food
____

3 soccer / yesterday
____

4 buy / a new cell phone / recently
____

5 book / last night
____

7 Answer the questions from activity 6 with information about yourself.

1 __________
2 __________
3 __________
4 __________
5 __________

8 Two friends are talking about a trip to Russia. Fill in the blanks to complete the conversation with tag questions.

Millennium of Russia, Veliky Novgorod

Ivan: Hey, Joe, I've heard you're going to Russia!

Joe: Yes! I'm so excited! You have been there, (1) __________?

Ivan: A long time ago, yeah. I visited my parent's city.

Joe: Your parents are from Moscow, (2) __________?

Ivan: In fact, they were born in Veliky Novgorod.

Joe: Oh, that's one of the most important historic cities in Russia, (3) __________?

Ivan: Yes, it is! You really did your homework, (4) __________?

Joe: I guess so. I've read a lot about all the cities I'm going to visit.

Ivan: You're not going to visit Magadan, (5) __________?

Joe: No, it's too far, (6) __________? I won't have the time!

Ivan: Yeah, you'd better focus on the major cities, like Moscow, Saint Petersburg and Veliky Novgorod.

Joe: They have great stories, (7) __________?

Ivan: Absolutely! You're going to have a lot of fun!

Extension

 Name: Class:

1 Complete the memes with *make* or *do*.

2 Look at the memes in activity 1 and answer the questions. Consider both image and text.

1 How does the person feel after exercising?

____

2 What happens when the girl tries to do her own hair? ______________________________

3 Is it easy to choose from many options? ______________________________

____

4 Why are the girls considered eccentric?

____

3 Use the words *do* or *make* to turn the images below into memes.

4 Check the correct word to complete the collocations.

1 Fariz ______ his creativity after the summer course.

a ☐ developed b ☐ raised

2 Good teachers ______ creativity.

a ☐ inhibit b ☐ encourage

3 My Art teacher doesn't give us much ______ for creativity. It should be the opposite, don't you think?

a ☐ house b ☐ room

4 There are several ways to ______ creativity.

a ☐ stimulate b ☐ refrain

5 Karine wants to develop her ______ creativity.

a ☐ artistic b ☐ skills

5 Complete the questions in the job interview. Use the simple past or the present perfect.

Interviewer: So, Genne, tell us a bit about yourself.

Genne: Well, I'm a blogger and I have written my blog since 2014.

Interviewer: And (1) ______________________

Genne: I have created memes for two years now.

Interviewer: (2) ______________________

Genne: I have created more than 100 memes already.

Interviewer: Wow! And (3) ______________________

Genne: No, I've never had any rights issues. I use free images and the texts are mine.

Interviewer: (4) ______________________

Genne: Yes, I created that meme. The sleeping cat is my favorite!

6 Circle the best option in each conversation.

1 **A:** Genne is arriving late from the interview, **is she** / **isn't she**?

B: Yeah, at 7 o'clock, I guess. You are not meeting her tonight, **are you** / **aren't you**?

2 **A:** Genne did well at her job interview, **did she** / **didn't she**?

B: She did. Anyway, she wasn't going to accept the offer, **was she** / **wasn't she**?

7 Look at the ad and fill in the blanks with *should*, *must*, *have to* or *can*.

1 You ______ have classes on Tuesdays or Thursdays.

2 You ______ go to the Community Center for the classes.

3 You ______ have a summer course certificate.

4 You ______ bring a notebook and colored pencils.

8 Match the sentence halves. Then write a continuation to each situation.

1 If Nancy goes to summer course,...

2 Donna would drive to the city...

3 If Ramirez learns Mandarin,...

4 You might stay up late...

5 If I took a creativity course,...

a [ ] if she had a license.
____

b [ ] if you have to finish the project.
____

c [1] she might need help with the housework.
If I help her, I won't have time to read my book.

d [ ] I would also learn how to be more confident.
____

e [ ] he can apply to the course he wants to take.
____

9 What might happen? Use the images below and write complete sentences.

1 

2 

3 

____

10 Use the second conditional and the prompts to write sentences about hypothetical situations.

1 study Art
____

2 go to college in another country
____

3 receive a prize
____

Extension